*The Arthur M. Okun Memorial Lecture Series*

# The
# Quiet
# Revolution

## Central Banking Goes

## Modern

*Alan S. Blinder*

*Foreword by Robert J. Shiller*

*Yale University Press*   *New Haven & London*

Set in Minion Roman types by Keystone Typesetting, Inc.

Printed in the United States of America.

*Library of Congress Cataloging-in-Publication Data*

Blinder, Alan S.

The quiet revolution : central banking goes modern / Alan S. Blinder; foreword by Robert J. Shiller.

p. cm. — (Arthur M. Okun memorial lecture series)

Includes bibliographical references and index.

ISBN 0-300-10087-6 (alk. paper)

1. Banks and banking, Central. I. Title. II. Arthur M. Okun memorial lectures.

HG1811.B554 2004

332.1′1—dc22                                                          2003061371

A catalogue record for this book is available from the British Library.

The paper in this book meets the guidelines for permanence and durability of the Committee on Production Guidelines for Book Longevity of the Council on Library Resources.

10  9  8  7  6  5  4  3  2  1

*To my wonderful wife, Madeline*

# Contents

# Illustrations

# Foreword

The "quiet revolution" that has taken place in central banking around the world in recent years represents changes in both procedure and substance. Alan Blinder describes changes in central bank procedures that underlie monetary policy: changes in public relations, in bureaucratic structure, and in the use of financial data. And yet, as he shows, the procedural changes are very much related to changes of substance, for the procedure influences the efficacy of monetary policy and answers some of the deepest concerns of central bankers.

Progress in the formulation of monetary policy appears to involve changes in procedure rather than in formulaic responses to economic conditions since the problem of maintaining an effective monetary policy is so subtle. There is fundamental uncertainty about the future course of the economy, about the public's interpretations of and reactions to monetary policy measures, and about possible political and social pressures. There is even disagreement about how to interpret basic monetary policy objectives. Because of these subtleties, central banking has widely been described as an art rather than a science.

In 1932, Sir Ralph Hawtrey gave an account of this subtlety in his

classic *The Art of Central Banking*. He argued that, despite fundamental uncertainty, central banking ought yet really to have a scholarly, if not a scientific, foundation: "But it is a special characteristic
of the art of central banking that it deals specifically with the task of
an authority directly entrusted with the promotion of human welfare. Human welfare, human motives, human behaviour supply material so baffling and elusive that many people are sceptical of the
possibility of building a scientific edifice on so shifting a foundation.
But however complex the material, and however imperfect the data,
there is *always* an advantage to be gained from systematic thought"
(R. G. Hawtrey, *The Art of Central Banking* [London: Longmans
Green, 1932], vi–vii). Professor Blinder's book is a perfect example
of the systematic thought that Hawtrey would have endorsed.

The progress that Blinder details in this book has perhaps been
slow, since the critical experiences, monetary crises, or economic
problems as well as the outcomes of central bank policies are themselves slow to reveal themselves. But the progress, informed as it has
been by both scholarly and practitioner insights, has been very important, ultimately, to human welfare. Blinder here shows an excellent feel for the nature of this progress, tying it to specific policy
concerns and to issues of economic theory.

One long-standing procedural problem for monetary policymakers is deciding what central bankers ought to tell the public. It is
a difficult problem because it is hard to say how we can expect the
public to react to central bank pronouncements. Since financial
market reactions are fundamentally tied to investor expectations,
and the functioning of the economy is connected with public confidence, central bankers have long perceived that they had best keep
their thinking a secret and issue only the most carefully worded
statements. Now, a consensus appears to be emerging that it is better
for central bankers to be open with the public. Blinder offers a

rationale for this consensus and some refinements about just what central bankers should be telling the public.

Another such problem for monetary policymakers is how to deal with the fundamental differences of opinion and objectives of people connected with the central bank itself. There is no agreement on an economic model, there is no agreement on the nature of economic conditions at any time, and there is no agreement even on how monetary policy success should be measured. Formulating good central banking policy requires some appreciation of the disagreement. It appears, from both practical evidence and experimental evidence that Blinder has created, that committees deal with the monetary policy problem better than individuals do and are not, as some have claimed. slow to react. The world's central banks are already heeding such evidence, and we are entering a time when central bankers are members of committees and administer policies that come not just from their own individual minds but instead from an interaction of many minds.

Yet another problem is discerning how much central bankers should respect the valuations expressed in financial markets. When Hawtrey wrote, central bankers often took a supercilious attitude toward these markets, acting as if they thought they had superior knowledge about the mass of herd behavior in the markets. Central bankers were then thought by many to be moral leaders as much as popes and philosophers. Many still view them in this way, but the mystique that central bankers have had has receded somewhat. Then the efficient markets revolution appeared in finance, and the efficient markets hypothesis took the academic profession by storm starting in the 1970s. In the 1990s, central bankers tended to respect markets too much, not even recognizing the stock market bubble of the 1990s, the biggest since the 1920s. Blinder here remarks on the advantages of respecting markets but then argues for a more balanced policy.

Overall, central banking has been getting much better through time. One might say that a new central banking technology has been evolving, for one can rightly call important procedures a technology, and these can make for better control of the world's economies. Personal judgment of market conditions will always play a fundamental role, but the way the judgment is translated into actions has been improved.

Blinder raised some of the difficult issues facing formulators of monetary policy in his earlier book *Hard Heads, Soft Hearts: Tough-Minded Economics for a Just Society* (Reading, Mass.: Addison-Wesley, 1987), and he gave there an important characterization of sensible and humane stabilization policy. He downplayed the importance of inflation relative to unemployment, asserting that a "gross misunderstanding blows the political importance of inflation out of all proportion to its economic importance" (51). He brought these views with him when he became vice-chairman of the U.S. Federal Reserve Board in 1994, and these led him into a bit of conflict with a strong and highly regarded Fed chairman, Alan Greenspan.

As detailed in the book by Bob Woodward, *Maestro: Greenspan's Fed and the American Boom* (New York: Simon and Schuster, 2000), Blinder learned at that time how difficult it can be to steer monetary policy in a new direction. Blinder not only resisted excessive tightening; he also pursued a new openness to monetary policy. He successfully advocated that the Federal Open Markets Committee should make a statement to accompany a decision to change interest rates, and he himself while vice-chairman flaunted precedent by discussing openly in public forums his views about monetary policy. But he quickly discovered the consequences of such actions when the institutional assumptions in the central bank do not support such candor and when the chairman is not fully behind it. Sensing the diminution of his influence as vice-chairman at the Fed, Blinder announced in 1996 that he would leave his post.

But he has not abandoned his commitment to fostering good monetary policy. Blinder's efforts to advance the cause of good monetary policy have led to new insights about the achievement of the ultimate objectives of monetary policy. This book will be remembered as an important treatise on the practice of central banking.

A word about the Okun Lecture series is in order. These lectures are named in honor of the late Arthur Okun, erstwhile Yale economics professor. Professor Okun, like Professor Blinder, entered Washington via the Council of Economic Advisers, and he, like Blinder, left his mark on Washington policymakers. Arthur Okun left Yale for a staff position on President Kennedy's Council of Economic Advisers in 1962. He became a council member in 1964, and chairman in 1966.

The anonymous donor for the Arthur Okun Memorial Lecture Series described his admiration for Arthur Okun and the intention of this lecture series in these terms:

> Arthur Okun combined his special gifts as an analytical and theoretical economist with his great concern for the well-being of his fellow citizens into a thoughtful, pragmatic, and sustaining contribution to his nation's public policy.
>
> Extraordinarily modest personally, he was a delightful and trenchant activist on behalf of others—both as members of our whole society and as individuals. He touched many, many people in ways they will always cherish.
>
> Offered in affectionate appreciation of Art's gifts, this lecture series seeks to recognize and encourage professional economists to search for policies that will contribute to the betterment of life and living.

Arthur Okun would have been fascinated by *The Quiet Revolution*, and it is a fitting addition to the series of Okun lectures.

Robert J. Shiller
Yale University

# Acknowledgments

I thank the economics faculty at Yale, especially Robert Shiller, for inviting and then prodding me to deliver the Okun Lectures in April 2002. When Bob approached me about the lectures in 2001, I was flattered but dubious. So I started thinking about two questions. First, having published a book of lectures on central banking (Blinder 1998) only three years earlier, did I have anything new to say? Second, did I have the time to write three lectures that were serious and substantial enough to pass muster with the sharp minds at Yale? I quickly concluded that the answer to the first question was yes— things had changed in the world of central banking—but that the answer to the second was probably no. Where would I find the time?

While mulling whether to opt for discretion or valor, I chanced to have a chat with the renowned finance economist Stephen Ross, who was at Princeton to deliver a set of lectures himself. Steve urged me to accept Yale's invitation with a simple argument: Committing to deliver the Okun Lectures would force me to make the time—and I would be glad that I did. I knew he was right. Sure enough, the hangman's noose concentrated the mind, and I showed up in New Haven in April 2002 with three lectures closely resembling what you find here.

All the folks at Yale were wonderfully hospitable and helpful during my three-day stay in New Haven, especially Bob Shiller's assistant, Carol Copeland. And while there, I benefited from a number of insightful comments both during and after the lectures from William Nordhaus, William Brainard, and others. Yale University Press then acquired two excellent reviewers, one of whom was Laurence Meyer (the other of whom was anonymous), whose valuable suggestions improved the manuscript further.

And, of course, I was fortunate to have the useful and perceptive observations of my Princeton colleagues Ben Bernanke (now a Federal Reserve governor), Christopher Sims, and Lars Svensson. Luke Willard provided truly excellent research assistance, and my assistant, Kathleen Hurley, took care of everything that needed to be done with her usual efficiency and good cheer. I am also grateful to Princeton's Center for Economic Policy Studies for financial support.

Finally, it was impossible for me, lecturing on monetary policy at Yale only about a month after James Tobin's death, not to think often about Yale's greatest macroeconomist since Irving Fisher. Like all macroeconomists of my generation, I admired Jim Tobin greatly. As I prepared these lectures, one of the things I was most looking forward to was Jim's trenchant but good-humored reactions to my ideas. That was going to be a special reward for me. But it was not to be.

*The Quiet Revolution*

# Introduction

Research on central banking is a growth industry. A computer search on the phrase "central banking," conducted on EconLit, turned up 980 references in the 1970s, 1,929 in the 1980s, and a staggering 4,921 in the 1990s. Performance like that does not quite match the stock market, but it is close. I will leave it to Bob Shiller to decide whether this growth reflects solid fundamentals or a faddish irrational exuberance.[1] But I will wager that the academic literature on central banking will not fall into a slump comparable to that of the Nasdaq.

In any case, all this quantitative growth has brought with it substantial qualitative change. About a decade ago, at a conference celebrating the Bank of England's tercentenary—yes, it's older than Yale!—Stanley Fischer (1994) presented a thoughtful and lengthy paper entitled "Modern Central Banking." Fischer's paper ran to forty-six published pages—in rather small type. It dealt with a wide variety of important topics. But it did not even mention two of the three issues that I will deal with in this book, and it barely touched on the third.

This observation is not meant as a criticism of Fischer, who was then as now a true expert and who produced a masterful, thought-provoking essay for the occasion. It is, rather, an indication of how much the times have changed in a scant ten years, even in the stodgy world of central banking.

The three issues that I have selected for this book are, in my judgment, among the most important facing central bankers today. Yet less than a decade ago, they barely registered on the radar screen of one of the world's foremost students of monetary policy. It is in that sense that thinking about how central banks should conduct their business has undergone changes that can aptly be termed *revolutionary*—although, as befits the discreet profession of central banking, the revolution proceeded quietly and has gone almost unnoticed.

## A Road Map

So what are these comparatively new issues? Chapter 1 is about *transparency*, the aspect of central banking in which change has probably been the most visible and dramatic over the past decade or so. About twenty years ago, the late Karl Brunner wrote the following biting caricature of the typical central banker's imperious attitude toward openness and transparency:

> Central Banking [has been] traditionally surrounded by a peculiar mystique. . . . The possession of wisdom, perception and relevant knowledge is naturally attributed to the management of Central Banks. . . . The relevant knowledge seems automatically obtained with the appointment and could only be manifested to holders of the appropriate position. The mystique thrives on a pervasive impression that Central Banking is an esoteric art. Access to this art and its proper execution is confined to the initiated elite. The esoteric nature of the art is moreover revealed by an inherent impossibility to articulate its insights in explicit and intelligible words and sentences.[2]

Now fast-forward to the present. In 2001, I was part of a five-author international team that wrote a detailed report on central bank transparency (Blinder et al. 2001). Inevitably, much of what I will have to say on that subject here overlaps considerably with that report; after all, my views did not change in the intervening months.[3] So when I lapse into the pronoun "we," I am referring also to my four coauthors. Here is how we opened our report: "Attitudes and policies toward central bank communications have undergone a radical transformation in recent years. Not long ago, secrecy was the byword in central banking circles. Now the unmistakable trend is toward greater openness and transparency. Increasingly, the central banks of the world are trying to make themselves understood, rather than leaving their thinking shrouded in mystery."[4] This represents quite a transformation from the world described by Brunner. I will argue in chapter 1 that it has been very much a change for the better—and that the trend ought to continue.

A second notable change in central banking practice has gone almost unremarked upon by theorists, despite its prominence in the real world of politics and institutions. So chapter 2 turns to the fascinating issue of whether monetary policy decisions are best made by an *individual* or by a *committee*. In the real world, there has been a clear trend in the way central banks organize themselves to conduct monetary policy: One-man rule used to be norm (and they *were* all men), but today most central banks make decisions by committee. The question is whether there are good reasons for this development—and what those reasons might be. Or, as they say, It works in practice; let's see if it also works in theory.

Finally, in chapter 3, I will turn to several aspects of the complex and evolving relationship between central banks and the financial markets. The question here, to put it rather too starkly, is, Who shall be servant, and who shall be master? I will argue that central banks, which used to pride themselves on lording it over the markets, have been showing them increasing deference in recent years. And I will ask whether this development should be viewed as a source of pride or a source of concern. My answer is, Both.

Each of these three issues will lead us to some knotty theoretical and empirical problems—*academic* research questions, you might call them. But each issue is also vitally important to the conduct of real-life monetary policy. I like to think that each raises the kind of questions that Art Okun might be wrestling with were he still alive— and it's a shame he's not. It was truly a privilege for me to deliver a series of lectures named in his honor.

# CHAPTER 1

# Through the Looking Glass: Central Bank Transparency

If there has been any storming of the Bastille during the quiet revolution in central banking, it has been the assault—mounted by some academics and a few central bankers—on the age-old notion that a central bank ought to be secretive and opaque. What happened to produce the sharp attitudinal changes I mentioned in the introduction? What are the main arguments in favor of greater transparency? And how can we evaluate the changes that have already taken place—and those yet to come? These are some of the main questions for this chapter. But first we must define our subject.

## What Is Transparency?

Academics have a fetish about precise definitions. So I began by consulting the dictionary for the definition of *transparency*. Mine (*Websters' Third New International Dictionary, Unabridged*) defines the word as dictionaries are wont to do: "the quality or state of being transparent." Not very helpful. Fortunately, among the three definitions of the adjective "transparent" that follow immediately are "free from pretense or deceit," "easily detected or seen through," and "readily understood." These will do. While I am personally attracted to the absence of pretense, that attribute seems extraneous to monetary transparency—and may not be terribly popular in central banking circles. So, for purposes of this book, I will say that a central bank is transparent if its actions are "easily detected," its policies are "readily understood," and its pronouncements are "free from deceit." In brief, the bank should be open, intelligible, and honest, in stark contrast to Karl Brunner's prototypical secretive, cryptic, and dissembling central bank.

To apply this general definition of *transparency* to the specific context of monetary policy, I begin by sketching a series of increasingly stringent transparency standards that a truly modern central bank might think of meeting. The easiest standard is *clarity*, or, as Brunner put it, articulating its views "in explicit and intelligible words and sentences." Asking only for this, and nothing more, is not asking for much. But as we know, even our own Alan Greenspan, whom I would rate as the greatest central banker in history, has often failed the clarity test. Examples abound. One of them occurred just a few months before I delivered the Okun Lectures. A speech Greenspan gave in San Francisco on January 11, 2002, created a stir when it was widely misinterpreted as conveying great concern with the strength of the economy and hinting that the Federal Open Market Committee (FOMC) might therefore cut interest rates once again at its next regularly scheduled meeting later that month.[1] Well, it turns out he was *not* all that worried about the recovery, and the FOMC was *not* thinking about cutting rates. The markets were clearly wrong-footed by Greenspan's speech, though presumably unintentionally. It was clarity that was lacking.

But clarity is not enough. If I declare forthrightly that I am standing at a podium in New Haven, Connecticut, wearing black socks, I haven't told you anything you don't already know—or care to know. So the second standard of transparency goes beyond clarity to *substantive content*. A central bank that is transparent by this more meaningful standard must convey pertinent information about the economy and monetary policy to those who care enough to listen. Here, a short personal anecdote is worth telling. I became vice chairman of the Federal Reserve Board in late June 1994. Within a few days, I had a visit from the Fed's longtime chief press officer, a fine man of deep experience who came to teach a rookie vice chairman the ropes. Trust me, his briefing was not intended to extol the virtues of transparency. In fact, at one point he informed me, "We don't talk about the economy." I looked at him incredulously and replied, with just a trace of sarcasm, "Then what would you like me to talk about? The weather?" Attitudes at the Fed (and elsewhere) have changed a lot since then.

The third standard of transparency raises the bar higher than mere substantive content. To clear this third hurdle, the central bank must leave itself *open to public scrutiny*. That need not and does not mean that its private records and internal memoranda must be posted on the Internet. But it does mean that the bank should provide the public with information about the nature of its deliberations, the reasoning behind its decisions (perhaps including some of the arguments pro and con), and the nature of the vote, if there is one. It probably also means that the bank should disclose most pertinent information about the inputs to its decision making, including both its model(s) and its forecasts. Only a few central banks meet this third standard.

Last, and to my mind least, the most demanding standard of transparency would require that substantially all of the central bank's business be *conducted in the sunshine*, free for all to see—the FOMC on CNBC, if you will. For reasons I will make clear shortly, my ideal central bank would meet the first three standards but not the fourth—which I believe to be unnecessarily intrusive, damaging to the deliberative process, and therefore potentially harmful to monetary policy. As we put it in our report on transparency (Blinder et al.

2001, 2), "The bank should reveal enough about its analysis, actions, and internal deliberations so that interested observers can understand each monetary policy decision as part of a logical chain of decisions leading to some objective(s)." That about sums it up. Transparency can and should stop short of voyeurism.

## The Political Case for Transparency

Although empirical evidence is notoriously hard to come by, there is a powerful a priori case for transparency in monetary policy. Succinctly stated, it comes down to this: that making the central bank more transparent both enhances democratic accountability and improves the quality of monetary policy.

Democratic accountability has not traditionally ranked high on the priority lists of central bankers, and in some cases it still does not. Milton Friedman once opined that central bankers' main goals are "avoiding accountability on the one hand and achieving public prestige on the other."[2] While Friedman was being a bit polemical, he had a point. It is an attitude that I always found difficult to square with democratic theory, and one that, thank goodness, has changed dramatically in recent years. More and more central bankers, and the governments that oversee them, have come to understand, first, that democratic accountability is a natural corollary of central bank independence and, second, that accountability requires transparency. Let me take up these two points in turn.

First, central banks in democratic countries exist not by divine right, but by authority of the government and therefore, as Jefferson might have put it, by the consent of the governed. Normally, the central bank is created by an act of the legislature or parliament and is accountable to it. The European Central Bank (ECB), by the way, is a notable exception to this rule. It was created by an international treaty, which is next to impossible to change, and it is not accountable to the government of any country. The ECB *is* required to report to the European Parliament, but it is in no sense a creature of that body—which in any case is hardly the seat of power in the European Union.

All this is very different in the United States. The Constitution assigned to Congress the power "to coin Money, [and] regulate the Value thereof," and Congress delegated this power to the Federal Reserve in 1913 by ordinary statute. It can therefore take the authority back any day it chooses. Indeed, while almost no one realizes it, Congress has the power to overrule any interest rate decision made by the FOMC by passing a statute that the president will sign. (It has, of course, never done so.)

By delegating authority over monetary policy to independent central bankers, elected officials grant them significant power over the economy and therefore over the lives and well-being of the populace. Certainly, few institutions in the United States have as much unfettered freedom of action as the Fed. Why do legislatures and parliaments voluntarily relinquish such authority? Presumably because they realize that independent central bankers with long time horizons provide a bulwark against inflation in a way that elected politicians cannot. So, at what might be called (figuratively, not literally) the "constitutional stage," lawmakers delegate authority over monetary policy to an independent central bank.[3]

In return for this broad grant of nearly unchecked authority, the central bank owes the legislature and the people a full and honest accounting of what it is up to and why. It should also, in principle, be punishable for failure and in some ultimate sense remain under political control. In the United States, political control is accomplished primarily in two ways. Congress, not the Fed, sets the basic goals of monetary policy, albeit loosely, and appointments to the

Federal Reserve Board are made by the president of the United States with the advice and consent of the Senate. The Fed is not a self-perpetuating oligarchy.[4]

Second, accountability requires transparency, including clarity about objectives. Interested parties cannot monitor the central bank's behavior if they cannot observe it. They cannot evaluate the quality of the banks' analysis and reasoning if that analysis and reasoning are not made available. And they cannot appraise the bank's success or failure if they do not know what it is trying to accomplish. I once suggested defining credibility as matching deeds to words.[5] Well, such a correspondence is impossible to establish if there are no "intelligible words and sentences" to be checked against the banks' actions.

I thus categorically reject the profoundly undemocratic view, which one nonetheless sometimes hears expressed, that transparency undermines central bank independence. The independence of the central bank should be protected not by secrecy, but by legal arrangements such as long terms of office for central bankers and statutory independence from political influence. Protections like that—plus the political will to make them stick—should enable central bankers to "take the heat" for even unpopular decisions to raise interest rates.

So the logical chain seems to me unbreakable: An independent central bank in a democracy must be accountable, and, to be accountable, a central bank must be transparent. We could perhaps stop the argument for transparency there and ask for a directed verdict. But there is also a powerful economic case.

## The Economic Case for Transparency

To begin at the beginning, I have long believed—contrary to what was once received central bank wisdom—that transparency enhances the efficacy of monetary policy rather than undermines it. The reason is simple. Central banks these days work their will by manipulating some very short-term interest rate—in the United States, the federal funds rate. But the funds rate is not an important price for any economic transactions of consequence; it merely clears the market in which reserves are lent overnight from one bank to another. The modern alchemy that transforms this dull lead into lustrous gold is that changes in the funds rate somehow influence the interest rates and asset prices that really matter, such as bank loan rates, corporate bond rates, home mortgage rates, stock prices, and exchange rates. But the gears connecting the funds rate to these more important interest rates and prices are sometimes quite loose, as I will emphasize in chapter 3. Tightening the gears would clearly make the effects of monetary policy on the economy more predictable and should therefore make the central bank more effective as a macroeconomic stabilizer.

But those gears are lubricated by *expectations,* which are notoriously slippery. Take the long-term bond rate as a concrete example. While the Fed controls only the funds rate, let's assume it would like to alter the ten-year bond rate.[6] According to the *expectations theory of the term structure,* which I will explain more fully in chapter 3, the ten-year rate depends on the sequence of one-day rates that are expected to prevail on each of the next 3,650 days or so. Those rates, in turn, depend on *future* monetary policy—in fact, in principle, they depend only on future monetary policy.[7] Thus *most* of the bond markets' *current* reaction to an FOMC decision should depend on how the market interprets the implications of that decision for future monetary policy. If an interest rate increase is expected to be quickly reversed, long rates should barely move. If, on the other hand, a rate hike engenders beliefs that further increases are on the way or that they will be long-lived or both, bond rates should rise sharply.

From the central bank's point of view, it is critical to anticipate how the market will react to its decisions because those reactions largely determine the ultimate effects of monetary policy on the economy. In my experience as a central banker, guessing how the markets would react to an FOMC decision was among our most difficult tasks. I imagine it is a bit easier today, however, because the Fed now makes much greater efforts to inform the markets and to condition market expectations of Federal Reserve policy.

As the Fed has offered a wider window into its thinking, and as the markets' understanding of the Fed has improved and deepened, market participants have grown more skilled at anticipating what the Fed will do. For example, Poole, Rasche, and Thornton (2001, esp. 29–31) offer empirical evidence that "the market has been able to better forecast Fed actions" (including being able to forecast further into the future) since the Fed began announcing its decisions immediately in February 1994. In principle, that enhanced ability should make the monetary policy transmission mechanism both more reliable and faster-acting.

Notice that the relationship is wonderfully symbiotic and, I believe, causal. The Fed gets better at predicting the market's reactions because the markets get better at predicting the Fed's policy decisions. And transparency—especially clear communication with the markets—is the key to the latter. As the market's ability to predict the Fed's monetary policy decisions improves, the lag between changes in monetary policy and changes in long-term interest rates should shorten.

A parallel point can be made about the expectations of future inflation that presumably influence wage- and price-setting behavior. Monetary policy will be more effective at managing inflation if wage and price setters understand what the central bank is up to and react accordingly.[8]

Lest these ideas seem banal, I hasten to point out that they run counter to what passed for received central bank wisdom not so very long ago. Secrecy, even mystery, was the byword, as the Brunner quotation in the introduction suggested. As late as 1993—hardly the Middle Ages—the Federal Reserve did not even disclose its monetary policy decisions at the time they were made. Instead of an official announcement, markets were forced to guess what the FOMC had *probably* decided—which gave professional Fed-watchers a clear advantage over amateurs.

In the bad old days, it was widely believed that central banks were supposed to catch markets "off guard" in order to manipulate them. And an important part of the canon was the dictum that a prudent central banker should never give *forward-looking* information. Well, the information that I have just characterized as *essential* is in fact forward-looking. How else can you influence expectations?

There are also more subtle ways in which greater transparency improves monetary policy. Consider this analogy. Most college teachers will tell you that you never truly master a subject until you teach it. There is something about the need to explain a complicated piece of analysis to a roomful of bright young people that concentrates the mind wonderfully. It helps—one might say, it forces—the teacher to notice and confront weak points in the reasoning, to resolve ambiguities, to bolster the arguments, and to understand better the arguments on the other side.

Similarly, a central bank that is forced to enunciate its goals, its basic strategy for achieving those goals, and the reasoning behind its specific decisions, all in ways that external observers can understand, will automatically and serendipitously impose a certain intellectual coherence on its internal deliberations. For example, as Laurence Meyer (2001), who left the Federal Reserve Board early in 2001, opined, "The internal discussion of policy would be more coherent if policymakers agreed in advance on an inflation objective." I could not agree more.

Conversely, a central bank board that cannot elucidate a clear rationale for its decision might well wonder whether its thinking is cogent and its decision is the right one. Sound policy is explicable; muddled policy often is not.

Modern economists would also mention the virtue of deepening the central bank's commitment to its goals by stating those goals publicly—a kind of Ulysses-to-the-mast effect. Possibly for this reason, greater transparency should make it easier for a central bank to alter its short-term tactics or even its medium-term strategy without engendering the belief that it has abandoned its long-term goals.

Furthermore, virtually all central bankers prize credibility, and transparency is one straightforward way to achieve it. After all, how can you demonstrate that you are true to your words if the only words you utter are inscrutable? A survey I did of eighty-four central bank heads a few years ago found that the vast majority rated credibility "of the utmost importance," and all the rest rated it "quite important," on a five-point scale that also included as choices "moderately important," "of minor importance," and "unimportant."[9] When it came to appraising ways to create or to maintain credibility, the central bankers ranked transparency right in the middle of a list of seven methods.[10]

Last but not least, greater transparency should also enhance and deepen public and legislative understanding of monetary policy, something that any honest central bank should welcome.

## Transparency About What?

The preceding arguments create a strong presumption in favor of disclosure. The burden of proof should always be on those who would withhold information; the "default option" should be revelation. But a burden of proof, as the lawyers will remind us, is only a rebuttable presumption. There are sometimes good reasons to insist on secrecy. For example, central banks must respect the confidentiality of proprietary information provided to them by commercial banks, of communications from other central banks and governments, and so on. Furthermore, some information is not pertinent: Alan Greenspan need not reveal his favorite websites nor his golf score. The objective should be transparency, not voyeurism. What, then, should a central bank reveal?

The report mentioned earlier (Blinder et al. 2001) lists three main categories of information: information about the central bank's *goals*, information about its *methods of analysis*, and information about its *decision-making processes*. Let's start with the goals of monetary policy, where full disclosure should be the almost-inviolable rule. For how can a central bank be held accountable if its goals are shrouded in mystery?

*Transparency About Goals*

A central bank's long-term goals are typically set forth in legislation, though perhaps only vaguely. It is the vagueness that raises the main transparency issue. I will briefly consider three cases, starting with one that leaves no ambiguity.

Inflation-targeting central banks have a single goal—low inflation; and they are normally given precise numerical targets by their governments. There is nothing wishy-washy about the Bank of Englands' mandate, which is to achieve 2.5 percent inflation, as measured by the Retail Price Index excluding mortgage interest rates. But most inflation targeters operate with a target range rather than a target point, which may create a bit of ambiguity. Is a central bank with a 1–3 percent range perfectly content when its inflation rate is 2.9 percent? Or does it want to nudge inflation down to 2 percent, the midpoint of its range? Most appear to aim for the midpoint, but they should say so. In general, however, inflation-targeting central banks face an easy test when it comes to goal transparency. And they pass it with flying colors.

There is some disagreement over whether the ECB should be classified as an inflation targeter in this sense. (I think it should be.) The ECB does have a single goal, but that goal is expressed vaguely in the treaty: "to maintain price stability." In an important step toward greater transparency, the ECB decided right away to define its goal precisely: an inflation rate between 0 and 2 percent, as measured by the "harmonized index of consumer prices." And since then it has further clarified that it prefers the upper end of that range. Since everyone who cares is aware of this numerical goal, it is a simple matter to hold the ECB accountable for achieving its inflation target.

Transparency poses a sterner test for the Federal Reserve and other central banks with multiple goals, especially when they are vaguely defined. The Federal Reserve Act directs the FOMC to pursue "maximum employment, stable prices, and moderate long-term interest rates." That complex legal mandate sets forth multiple goals and falls far short of specifying concrete objectives for monetary policy.[11] What is meant by "maximum employment"? What measured inflation rate constitutes "stable prices," and by what price index? How is one goal to be traded off against another? The Fed has steadfastly refused to answer any of these questions, except in the vaguest terms. For example, using the Feds' current favorite price index, the deflator for core personal consumption expenditures, inflation averaged 1.6 percent over the four quarters just preceding my Okun Lectures. Was that above or below the Feds' long-run objective? No one outside the Fed knew then or knows now. In fact, opinions probably differed even inside the Fed because the FOMC has never quantified its inflation target—not even internally.[12] I believe not only that it should do so, but also that it should announce the number publicly. (These are two different questions.)

Defining the employment target is trickier. The phrase "maximum employment" cannot be taken literally, given that the Fed also has a price stability objective. Driving the unemployment rate down to World War II levels, for example, would surely ignite inflation. One reasonable interpretation, and the one that seems to guide FOMC thinking, would define the employment goal as pushing the unemployment rate down to the natural rate (if there is one), but not lower—that is, achieving the highest level of employment consistent with constant (and presumably low) inflation. As Meyer (2001, 9) recently noted, turning that concept into a specific number that the FOMC would announce is difficult.[13] But "that does not rule out . . . being more transparent about their estimate of the unemployment rate that is consistent with maximum sustainable employment." I agree. The Fed's practice leaves much room for improvement.

Having said that, however, I should acknowledge that the distinction between an inflation-targeting central bank and one with multiple objectives like the Fed is not quite as sharp as I have suggested so far. As many advocates of inflation targeting have pointed out,[14] an inflation targeter that is willing to approach its target *gradually* also has an implicit output stabilization objective, albeit a vague one (unless the speed of approach is stated publicly and numerically).

*Transparency About Methods*

Questions also arise, and practices differ, over how much central banks should reveal about the analysis that presumably underpins their policy decisions, especially their forecasts and their models. As a broad generalization, I think it is fair to say that central banks have been reluctant to tell too much. But practices have been changing, and the current trend is clearly toward more disclosure—a trend that should be both applauded and continued, in my view. To avoid tedium, I will deal only with forecasts; but similar principles apply to transparency about models.

Everyone knows that macroeconomic forecasts are not terribly accurate. But everyone also knows that they are indispensable to monetary policy making. Given the long lags, there is little choice but to act on the basis of a forecast, however fallible. So every central bank makes forecasts, generally quite frequently. The Federal Reserve staff prepares a complete, detailed forecast for every scheduled FOMC meeting—eight times a year. The question is, Should these forecasts be made public? By now you can guess that my answer is yes. The reasons are many, and three merit a brief mention.

First comes the basic presumption that all pertinent information should be disclosed unless there is a persuasive reason to withhold it. The bank's forecast is surely pertinent. Is there any good reason to keep it secret? I think not, other than the potential embarrassment when forecasts turn out to be wrong. But using inaccuracy as an excuse for secrecy is tantamount to denying that the central bank should be held accountable. Objection sustained.

A variant of this argument sounds better, at least superficially: A series of poor published forecasts might undermine the banks' credibility and thereby hamper its ability to conduct policy. But markets are surely sophisticated enough to realize that macroeconomic forecasts often miss the mark. Only a central bank whose forecasts were systematically worse than the consensus would lose credibility—and in that case, it should. In fact, however, Romer and Romer (2000) found that the Fed's staff forecasts were consistently better than private sector forecasts. So this argument backfires on defenders of the Fed's tradition of secrecy. Besides, knowing that the central bank acted on an erroneous forecast might sometimes help explain monetary policy decisions that otherwise look wrong-headed with the magnificent wisdom of hindsight.

A second reason to reveal the central bank's forecast harkens back to my earlier discussion of the virtues of conditioning market expectations. One simple way to get the markets thinking more like the Fed would be for the Fed to publish its forecasts of the economy. Were the Fed to do so, market participants who were trying to predict interest rates would quickly embrace the Fed's forecasts as far more relevant than their own. After all, the Fed (a) presumably acts on its own beliefs and (b) has at least some (albeit limited) power to make its forecasts come true.

A third and related reason is educational. The central bank can explain its actions to the public better if it uses its forecast as a backdrop: "This is what we expected to happen, so this is what we did." For example, when the Bank of England's "fan chart" shows that inflation will probably rise above 2.5 percent under unchanged monetary policy, that forecast establishes the predicate for higher interest rates.

One objection that central bankers occasionally raise is that the staff's forecast may not correspond to the beliefs of the actual decision makers.[15] My answer is, So what? A large committee (the FOMC has nineteen members) cannot possibly agree on a detailed forecast, so it is of interest to see what the staff is telling it. More important in the U.S. context, a large portion of every FOMC meeting is devoted to an "economy round," in which committee members state and explain how and why they agree or disagree with the staff forecast. Were this discussion summarized in the published minutes along with the staff forecast, they would together convey a quantum of useful information to interested observers.

So once again, my answer is unequivocal. A transparent central bank should reveal the broad contours of its internal (typically, staff) forecasts as often as they are made. Notice the phrase "broad contours." The Fed's Greenbook, for example, contains quarterly forecasts of literally scores of variables. But the market could not care less about the Fed's forecast of, say, multifamily housing starts in the fourth quarter of 2004 or the trade deficit in services in the first quarter of 2005. It wants to know what the Fed thinks about the likely evolution of real GDP, employment, the inflation rate, and a few other key variables.

Transparency about the forecast does, however, lead to one very difficult issue. Any macroeconomic forecast that stretches beyond a quarter or two must embody some assumptions about future monetary policy. That is understandably considered a rather delicate subject for a central bank to speculate about in public, although the Reserve Bank of New Zealand (RBNZ) seems to manage it just fine. The monetary authorities appear to have three main options.

The most obvious one is to publish a forecast conditional on no further changes in short-term interest rates, even if the bank actually expects to be changing rates in the future. That is not only a clean solution, it is also likely to reveal the need for an adjustment of policy—and so need not be thought of as deceptive. But neither is it 100 percent honest. And assuming that short rates will remain constant can lead to inconsistent forecasts of, for example, long rates, since long-term interest rates presumably embody the markets' expectations of future monetary policy changes—and those expectations will often include some expected changes in monetary policy.[16]

The opposite extreme is to adopt the RBNZs policy, which is to project its own behavior over the forecast horizon—subject, of course, to numerous provisos. This practice raises transparency to a level that few central bankers are comfortable with, and the RBNZ has no emulators that I know of. Nor is it really practical for most central banks at present, since hardly any of them make even tentative judgments about what their future monetary policy decisions will be.[17] One might argue that they *should* do so; indeed, I have made that very argument.[18] But the fact is that they do not. At least for now, the almost-universal rule is: Let's take it one meeting at a time.

An intermediate option is to use market expectations of what the central bank is likely to do—which is, of course, precisely what private sector forecasters do all the time. Every major central bank can follow this procedure if it wishes to since there are objective financial market readings of what traders expect them to do. Well, almost. In truth, different markets do not always agree, and there is more than one "consensus forecast." Furthermore, the market's macroeconomic forecast may differ from the central bank's. Alas, it's an imperfect world.

A true transparency hawk like me might long for the day when more central banks will follow the lead of the "extremists" in New Zealand. But, in the meantime, I would be content to see the Fed and other central banks meet the *lowest* of these three transparency standards: publishing *staff* forecasts based on *unchanged* short-term interest rates as often as those forecasts are prepared. That alone would be a great leap forward. In fact, armed with such a forecast and knowledge of the central bank's goals and procedures, astute outside observers ought to be able to forecast future monetary policy decisions pretty well. No one would misinterpret the central bank's assumption of constant interest rates as a true forecast of its future behavior.

*Transparency About Decisions and Decision Making*

It may seem self-evident that a central bank should announce its monetary policy decisions as soon as they are made—if for no other reason than to avoid giving professional central bank watchers an unfair advantage. But, as I noted earlier, the FOMC steadfastly refused to do even this until February 1994.

Reading the Fed's tortured defense of its indefensible position from today's perspective is a bit like reading medieval scholastic dogma. But as late as 1989 Chairman Greenspan told a House committee that requiring the Fed to announce its interest rate decisions immediately "would be ill-advised" and "could impede timely and appropriate adjustments to policy."[19] In answer to a subsequent written question submitted by a committee member, he explained why. His answer ran to three long, strained paragraphs that I will not bore you with here. But it included the astonishing (from a contemporary perspective) notion that the Fed might want to conceal its policy change in order to forestall "outsized market reactions"[20]— this from a man who believes in the wisdom of markets and disapproves of the nanny state. The sentiment reminds me of the climactic line from the play *A Few Good Men* when the accused marine officer screams at the prosecuting attorney, "You can't handle the truth!"

Nowadays, of course, immediate announcements are no longer an issue at the Fed—or anywhere else. Virtually all central banks make their decisions public right away. But there are sharp differences over how deeply outsiders are allowed to peer inside the decision-making process. Here are three representative examples, arranged from least to most transparent:

- The ECB maintains that all interest rate decisions are made by consensus—presumably by unanimity—and that votes are never taken. But there are skeptics. Can deciding on a uniform monetary policy for twelve countries with disparate macroeconomic conditions really be that easy? Are there never dissenters on the other side? (Press reports have frequently suggested that there sometimes are.) Nor does the ECB ever publish minutes that might teach outsiders something about the nature of the internal debate.
- The FOMC has long disclosed how each member voted and recently began to do so immediately. But the statements that accompany each decision are extremely terse, sometimes cryptic, and reveal little about the arguments that were made at the meeting—or even about the ones that prevailed. Fortunately, the FOMC minutes, which are published six to seven weeks later, do convey some sense of the arguments pro and con—though they could say a lot more. And the Fed stands virtually alone in publishing verbatim transcripts of its meetings five years later.[21]

- The Bank of England is the most open of the three. Its Monetary Policy Committee (MPC) publishes detailed minutes that make the nature of the debate clear with only about a two-week delay.

By now, it will surprise no one to learn that I prefer the Bank of England's model. A monetary policy committee should not emulate the college of cardinals sending up smoke through chimneys. Nor are its meetings grand jury proceedings. After redacting any confidential material that may come up (which is a comparatively easy task), all the major substantive points raised in the discussion can be, and I believe should be, made public. Verbatim transcripts, however, go a step too far, in my view, as they are likely to limit frankness and everyday banter, prevent people from taking "devil's advocate" positions, and otherwise stifle debate. They tend to produce script reading, which satisfies the classic definition of a lecture: The process by which the notes of the professor are transferred to the notebook of the student, without passing through the mind of either.

The most difficult transparency issue within the realm of decision making is essentially the same one we dealt with in the case of transparency about forecasts. Suppose the monetary policy committee, at a particular meeting, decides not only on today's monetary policy, but also makes a tentative plan—whether vague or specific— for future monetary policy. Should those tentative plans be revealed to the public? On this question, too, there has been substantial evolution in mainstream central bank thinking in recent years.[22]

The traditional view held that a central bank should scrupulously avoid tipping its hand. So, for example, until May 1999 the Federal Reserve kept the "bias" in its directive secret until after the following FOMC meeting—by which time it was irrelevant. In part, this attitude was justifiable—after all, it could be misleading to "inform" markets about decisions that might never be taken—although one wonders, with Karl Brunner, whether this was the real justification for such secrecy.

In any case, an alternative view has gained the ascendancy in recent years. It holds that a central bank ought to tell markets, politicians, and the general public which way it is leaning. The Fed has been doing this in a formal way since May 1999 with a "balance of risk" sentence stating whether the FOMC is more concerned with inflation or weakness in the economy going forward (the balance of risk assessment was expanded in 2003 to include separate evaluations of inflation risk and real growth risk). The ECB has been doing almost the same thing, albeit a bit less formally, at the president's press conferences that generally follow meetings of the Governing Council. Even when there is no explicit bias announcement, revealing the monetary policy committee's vote may carry a strong hint about where interest rates might head in the future. A 5–4 vote on the Bank of England's MPC, for example, conveys rather different information than a 9–0 vote.

Is it possible—and advisable—to go even further? As mentioned earlier, the RBNZ is the only central bank that does. Since June 1997, it has published a contingent three-year plan for future monetary policy. The RBNZ emphasizes that policy settings for the future are merely "projected"—and conditional on evolving circumstances. Should other central banks follow New Zealand's lead and offer more explicit guidance about the likely path of future short-term interest rates? There are coherent arguments on both sides.

On the one hand, I have argued repeatedly here and in the introduction that the monetary authorities should reveal as much as possible and keep market participants well informed. Such arguments apply to future as well as to present monetary policy. Indeed, when we speak of conditioning market expectations, it is largely expectations about future monetary policy that we have in mind. Announcing the bias in the central bank's current policy stance and explaining the concerns that led to that bias (as the Federal Reserve does in part) is one way to pursue this objective. But announcing the bank's current beliefs about what future monetary policy might be, provided things evolve according to the forecast (as the RBNZ does), would give the market even more relevant information. The pure logic of transparency surely pushes us in this direction.

But there are also some practical arguments on the other side. Most important is the point I made earlier: We cannot ask central banks to reveal information they do not have; and, for better or worse, almost none of them currently formulate contingent plans for future monetary policy—not even for internal use. Even if the central bank does formulate such plans, it is all but certain that the future will not unfold as anticipated, and central bankers do not relish changing their minds in public. Documented errors in forecasting would, after all, undermine the doctrine of central bank infallibility! More important (and more seriously), the monetary policy that is actually followed in the future will almost certainly differ from the announced (contingent) future policy path. So defenders of the status quo can argue that announcing a tentative future path does not actually convey much useful information. (I disagree.)

Perhaps the best a central bank can do is to "teach" the market its way of thinking. Then market participants can process incoming data in more or less the same way as the central bank does and adjust their own forecasts of monetary policy accordingly. As suggested earlier, a forecast that inflation will rise if nominal interest rates are held constant may "look and feel" like an implicit forecast that the bank will have to raise rates before too long. And that belief will presumably get embodied in long-term interest rates.

## Delivering the Message: Methods of Communication

Once a central bank has decided what information it will reveal, it must next figure out how best to do so. There are five main vehicles for delivering information to the public, and most of them have already been mentioned: the statements that accompany policy decisions, the so-called "bias announcements," the minutes of committee meetings, official tabulations of votes, and testimony and speeches by members of the MPC. The most appropriate mix of these various modes of communication depends sensitively on the institutional setting—especially on how monetary policy decisions are reached. So I need a typology first.[23]

At some central banks, for example the RBNZ and, for the most part, the Bank of Canada, decision-making authority still rests with one individual, the governor.[24] But increasingly individual decision makers are giving way to committees—as I will discuss in chapter 2. Here a further distinction is necessary, one to which I will return in the next chapter.

Some monetary policy committees, such as the Fed's FOMC and the ECB's Governing Council, might be called "collegial"—meaning that they strive to reach decisions by consensus, with or without a formal vote. Individual members are expected to fall in line behind the group's decision, and accountability resides in the group. But other MPCs, such as the Bank of England's and the Swedish Riksbank's, are much more "individualistic"—meaning that members are expected to express and presumably vote for their own preferred policy choice, much like justices of the U.S. Supreme Court do. And much like the justices, each individual is held accountable for his or her own vote.

Reasons for the observed shift from individual to group decision making at central banks, and the relative merits of reaching decisions in each of these three ways, are among the fascinating questions for the next chapter. For now, let's focus on a narrower question: How should information be conveyed under each of the three systems?

The case of an individual decision maker is the simplest. Since there is no committee meeting, there are clearly no minutes nor any vote to report. This places the burden of explaining the central bank's thinking squarely on the statement that accompanies each policy announcement. These statements should therefore be coherent, well-reasoned, and sufficiently detailed to explain why the governor decided as he did. If the central bank maintains a bias going forward, that too should be revealed in the statement. All this can and should be amplified in subsequent testimony and speeches. Pretty simple—though, as Brunner noted, not an integral part of long-standing central banking tradition.

With decision making by committee, the communication task becomes immensely more complicated, for many reasons. But the principal issue can be stated as a simple question: How do you handle disagreements within the committee?

In a truly collegial committee, which is roughly the system in the EU and perhaps in the United States,[25] there is some justification for submerging differences, at least in public. After all, the group's decision is supposed to have emerged from some mythical "collective mind" after a careful weighing of the various pros and cons. In principle, if not in fact, everyone on the committee shares ownership of the decision, and the committee should therefore be able to speak with one voice—at least to outsiders.

On the other hand, when monetary policy decisions are made by an individualistic committee, differences of opinion are an essential component of transparency. Different viewpoints and even multiple voices are welcome because they help to reveal the underlying reality. As such, they are more likely to enlighten than to confuse outside observers.

Thus, for example, announcing the vote after each policy meeting is an essential aspect of transparency in an individualistic committee like those of the Bank of England and Sweden's Riksbank. In such cases, the numerical vote is likely to be a useful indicator of how the central bank is balancing the competing considerations. But in collegial settings like that of the ECB's Governing Council, it may be justifiable to suppress the vote—or at least to suppress the names of individual voters—in the interest of maintaining group harmony.[26]

The Fed is a hybrid in this respect. These days it reports each vote immediately, naming names. But the vote does not always reflect the true preferences of committee members because of a long-standing tradition that a member of the FOMC should vote to support the chairman's recommendation unless he or she disagrees with it very strongly. Tellingly, votes against the majority position are called "dissents," and they are relatively rare.[27]

Next, after votes, comes the statement accompanying each policy decision. I believe there should always be one, even when the decision is to leave interest rates unchanged. Announcing your interest rate decision without giving any supporting reasons suggests an imperious attitude that, while possibly appropriate for emperors, is certainly inappropriate for public servants in a democratic society. The Fed took a long time to come around to the view that "no change" is a decision just like any other—a view I tried unsuccessfully to promote while I was the Fed's vice chairman—but it now issues a short statement on such occasions. The Bank of England normally does not, however.

How much needs to be said immediately in the statement versus later in the minutes probably differs between collegial and individualistic committees. A collegial committee should be prepared to issue a substantive statement explaining its reasoning in "intelligible words and sentences" as soon as its policy decision is announced, which should be shortly after the meeting ends. When I was on the FOMC, it was often argued that it could take hours to get nineteen people to agree on a statement—and this argument is still heard today. But a skillful chairman can walk into a room with a draft of the statement in hand and then modify it as necessary (probably only slightly) to reflect the sense of the meeting. So I see this objection as more of an excuse than a serious barrier.

Important aspects of the central bank's reasoning and arguments that are *not* disclosed in the immediate statement should be disclosed in the subsequent minutes. If a collegial committee releases a statement with real substantive content after each meeting, then the detailed minutes—which come out much later—may not be of much interest to market participants. Indeed, even the very sparse press statements provided after each FOMC meeting seem to convey enough information that release of the detailed minutes six to seven weeks later (just after the next meeting) normally elicits very little press coverage and negligible market reaction. Nonetheless, I think the FOMC minutes could and should be made more readable and useful.

The situation is quite different with an individualistic committee. Meetings of the Bank of England's MPC often end with no consensus on either the decision itself (which is taken by majority vote) or the reasons behind it. Reportedly, meetings are often freewheeling affairs, quite unlike the FOMC's staid and ultrapolite conclaves. At the end of such a debate, it may be difficult to draft a meaningful statement to accompany the announcement; so the Bank of England rarely does so. I think they need to try harder; after all, the Bank of Japan manages to do it. But regardless, the primary vehicle for disclosure by an individualistic committee will probably be the minutes, which should therefore be published as soon as possible. These days, that happens after about a two-week delay at the Bank of England; and there is evidence that the markets react (at least slightly) to publication of the minutes.[28]

At some, but not all, central banks, either the immediate statement or the subsequent minutes state the bank's "bias" or its perception of the "balance of risks" going forward. This recent innovation flies in the face of the age-old dogma that central banks should never give forward-looking information about monetary policy. It is also a big improvement. As I noted previously, providing such information is an excellent way to condition market expectations, which is a primary purpose of transparency.

## The Special Case of Inflation Targeting

Inflation targeting is typically practiced with a high degree of transparency. Inflation-targeting central banks normally announce their numerical inflation target, publish explicit inflation forecasts, and issue lengthy "inflation reports" with much analysis and supporting detail. Indeed, proponents of inflation targeting often cite its extreme transparency as one of its most distinctive features and primary virtues. For example, Bernanke, Laubach, Mishkin, and Posen (1999, 10) write that, in their view, the "most essential" rationale for inflation targeting is that it "helps policy-makers to communicate their intentions to the public and to impose some degree of accountability and discipline on the central bank."

In this regard, a recent attempt to rank nine central banks from highest to lowest in terms of transparency seems to reach a surprising conclusion. The authors claim to find "remarkable variation in overall transparency among central banks that have adopted inflation targeting."[29] Of the nine central banks they study, however, five are explicit inflation targeters (the Reserve Bank of Australia, the Bank of Canada, the Reserve Bank of New Zealand, the Swedish Riksbank, and the Bank of England); and four of these five rank among the top five in transparency.[30] That's a pretty good correlation. And knowing the histories of each bank, I would say the correlation is no accident. Both commitment to a specific inflation target and a quantum leap in transparency were parts of an institutional design package intended to build credibility very rapidly.

But is greater transparency, in and of itself, a sufficient reason to adopt inflation targeting? Despite the high value I place on openness and communication, I am not personally convinced it is. I fear that, in the U.S. context at least, a switch to inflation targeting would automatically downgrade the importance of the Fed's employment (or output stabilization) goal. Indeed, how else could such a rewrite of the Federal Reserve Act be interpreted?[31] I have long applauded the Fed's distinctive dual mandate and admired Alan Greenspan's skillful use of it. Both have stood the country in good stead. The starkly different legal mandates of the ECB and the Fed have, I believe, allowed Greenspan to gamble on growth in a way that the more cautious ECB (and the Bundesbank before that) was unwilling to do. This is one, though not the only, reason the United States outperformed Europe in the 1990s.[32]

Supporters of inflation targeting will object to my objection on several grounds. They will insist that I exaggerate the difference between *flexible* inflation targeting and the Fed's dual mandate, because flexible inflation targeting does not imply that the central bank has no concerns about short-run employment.[33] Instead, they will say, the stance of monetary policy should be truly symmetrical—equally opposed to inflation that is too low as to inflation that is too high. They might also point out that competent inflation targeting provides a natural safeguard against settling for an unemployment rate that is too high, say, because economists overestimate the natural rate. Even if no one knows what the natural rate of unemployment is, inflation should be falling as long as unemployment remains above it—thereby signaling the central bank to ease.[34]

This is all true. But optics matter in the real world of policy. I doubt that the Fed would have permitted such vigorous growth in the 1990s if its mandate had been, say, to bring inflation down to 1 or 2 percent—period. In a world of low inflation, I also worry that inflation targeters will not be as adept at fighting *de*flation as they are at fighting *in*flation.[35] Once inflation is allowed to dip into (or near) negative territory, monetary stimulus loses much of its punch because of the zero lower bound on nominal interest rates.[36] That is one reason why missing a 1 percent inflation target by two percentage points on the low side is, in my view, worse than missing by two percentage points on the high side.

And last, but certainly not least, we should not forget the first principle of institutional conservatism: If it ain't broke, don't fix it. It would take a great deal to convince me that U.S. monetary policy since 1979—that's twenty-four years, under two Fed chairmen—would have been better if only we had instituted inflation targeting back then and stuck with it through thick and thin. On the other hand, one might legitimately argue that a time span in which Alan Greenspan succeeds Paul Volcker at the helm is a bit like the New York Yankees' good fortune in being able to replace Joe DiMaggio with Mickey Mantle in centerfield. You cannot expect to do that consistently. (And the Yankees did not.)

## The Moving Finger Writes and, Having Writ, Moves On

Central bank transparency is a moving target. The bad news is that the Federal Reserve is not nearly as open and communicative as it should be—it is far from the vanguard in terms of transparency.[37] What is left on the Fed's transparency agenda? Quite a lot, I would say. Ultimate targets should be decided upon and enunciated more clearly; forecasts should be published; statements should be longer and less cryptic; minutes should be clearer and more descriptive.

But the good news is that, like many other central banks, the Fed is moving unmistakably in the right direction.[38] While the worldwide migration of central banks toward greater transparency has been gradual, cumulatively it constitutes a near-revolution in central bank thinking and practice. In a real sense, the world that Karl Brunner plaintively described in 1981 no longer exists. And almost all of the progress has taken place in the past decade or so.

I will be so bold—or so foolish, take your pick—as to conclude this chapter with a prediction: The unmistakable movement of the world's central banks in the direction of more, and more honest, communication is both irreversible and unstoppable. Once a step toward greater transparency is taken, it is well-nigh impossible to step back in the other direction—which may be why foes of transparency occasionally dig in their heels so deeply to preserve the status quo.

But such rearguard actions are doomed to failure. Opening the door to greater transparency is a bit like opening Pandora's box—but only in the sense that you cannot get it closed again. The nice thing is that central banks almost never want to. The experience in one country after another shows that each experiment with an aspect of transparency previously thought "unthinkable" quickly leaves central bankers wondering why they had not taken the step sooner. Here, at least, there appears to be no conflict between theory and practice. Transparency works wonderfully well in both domains.

# CHAPTER 2

# Ex Uno Plures:
# Central Banking by Committee

Economics is the science of *individual* choice. Ever since the days of Adam Smith, economists have glorified the ability of individuals to reach decisions that best serve their own interests. The stereotypical hero of economics is the lone-wolf entrepreneur who is guided, as if by an invisible hand you might say, to the right conclusions even though others may insist that he is wrong—just the sort of person Ayn Rand had in mind when she created Howard Roark. So it is hardly surprising that virtually all theories of central bank behavior model the central bank as a single optimizer minimizing a well-defined loss function subject to constraints—the canonical problem of microeconomics.

Yet we all know that society assigns many important decisions to groups rather than to individuals. Legislatures, of course, make the laws; juries decide cases; and so on. Corporations have boards of directors (in addition to CEOs). The U.S. Supreme Court is a committee that makes decisions by majority vote. There are presumably reasons to prefer groups over individuals in certain contexts. Could monetary policy be one of those contexts? That, essentially, is the central question of this chapter.

## Many, From One

This chapter jumps off from a fascinating fact mentioned in the introduction that has apparently escaped the notice, or at least the attention, of almost all economists who do research on central banking. Whereas decision making by committee used to be the exception in monetary policy—the Fed and the Bundesbank being the primary examples—it has now become the *rule*. In its *Guide to Central Bank Watching for 2000*, J. P. Morgan (2000, 4) observed that "one of the most notable developments of the past few years has been the shift of monetary policy decision-making to meetings of central bank policy boards, often loosely fashioned after the U.S. Federal Reserve's open market committee (FOMC). Twenty-nine of the 34 central banks covered in this publication have a monetary policy committee (or MPC) that sits with the explicit mandate of setting monetary (generally interest-rate) conditions." Since three of the other five were currency boards with no monetary policy decisions to make, that left only two central bank heads—in Norway and New Zealand—as individual decision makers.[1]

Thus one of the hallmarks of the quiet revolution in central banking practice has apparently been a movement toward making decisions by committee, whereas previously the dictatorial central bank governor was more the norm. Recent years have seen the United Kingdom, Sweden, Switzerland, and Brazil, for example, move in this direction; and most of the twelve central banks that were absorbed into the European System of Central Banks were formerly run by individual governors. I am not aware of any transitions in the opposite direction—from committees to individuals. Such a clear trend in institutional design raises a simple and obvious question: Why have so many central banks switched from individual to group decision making?

It is easy to exaggerate the difference between the two organizational structures, and we must not fall into that trap. The FOMC, for example, putatively makes monetary policy decisions by majority vote. But in fact it is widely recognized that the committee generally ratifies the decisions of its chairman, Alan Greenspan. The vote is almost always a formality and is normally unanimous. For example, in the thirty-five FOMC meetings spanning the four full years 1998–2001, there were only eleven officially recorded dissents.

On the other hand, it is equally mistaken to ignore the differences between central banks that make monetary policy decisions by committee and those that do not. Prior to 1998, for example, the Bank of England's interest rate decisions were made unilaterally by its then-governor, Eddie George. (Prior to that, the bank was not independent, and monetary policy was made by the chancellor of the exchequer.) Now they are made by a nine-person Monetary Policy Committee (MPC) that apparently argues like the Oxford–Cambridge Debating Society and decides on monetary policy by genuine majority vote. The governor's voice seems to be just one among equals on a truly democratic committee. Even at the very *un*democratic Fed, Chairman Greenspan sometimes must tack to keep his fellow committee members on board.

In this respect, as in so many others, life is more nearly continuous than dichotomous. Imagine a continuum with purely autocratic rule on one end of the spectrum and purely democratic decision making on the other (see fig. 2.1). Central banks are distributed across this continuum with, say, the Reserve Bank of New Zealand on the extreme left and the Bank of England on the extreme right. The fascinating fact that motivates this chapter is that the weight of the empirical distribution has shifted noticeably to the right in recent years, toward more group decision making.

Prior to my Marshall Lectures at Cambridge in 1995, in which I pointed this out and suggested that it might matter for monetary

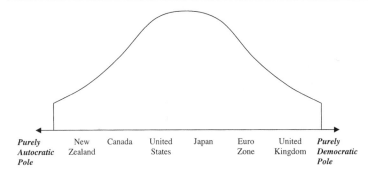

| *Purely* | New | Canada | United | Japan | Euro | United | *Purely* |
| *Autocratic* | Zealand | | States | | Zone | Kingdom | *Democratic* |
| *Pole* | | | | | | | *Pole* |

**Figure 2.1**   Autocracy vs. Democracy at Central Banks

policy, there was virtually no theorizing about central banks as committees.[2] Scores of papers had been written on the false premise that the distribution of central banks in figure 2.1 was piled up at the autocratic pole. The literature treated monetary policy decisions as solutions to optimization problems solved by a single individual— just as a consumer maximizes utility or a firm minimizes cost. This was and is plainly incorrect. But is the theoretical oversight consequential? Do group decisions differ systematically from individual decisions? And, if so, which arrangement should society prefer at its central bank? Questions like these were rarely even asked before 1998. But since then a few papers addressing the issue have appeared in print. I proceed now to summarize what they have to say. Since there are only a few, this summary will not take up much space.

## Individuals versus Committees: Theory

But first, two preliminary points. The first is to note that, in many countries, the movement from an individual central banker to a committee went hand-in-glove with granting independence to the central bank. The reason is clear enough. When the central bank was just doing the government's bidding, there was not much point in having a committee to make monetary policy. What, after all, would a committee deliberate about? But once independence was granted, the choice between an individual and a committee became a real one. That brings me to the second point.

If *Homo sapiens* behaved like *Homo economicus*, it would not matter whether decisions were made by an individual or by a committee. Since every member of a committee of *homines economici* would see the same data and process it in the same way, they would all reach the same conclusions. Every committee vote would therefore be unanimous, and the committee's decisions would be identical to what any single member, acting alone, would have done.[3]

In reality, however, members of a monetary policy committee frequently reach different conclusions. There are several reasons for this. To begin with, economic theorists like to build models in which agents receive different, somewhat idiosyncratic, information. In some decision-making problems, differential information is essential. But you can mostly ignore it in the monetary policy context because virtually all the data that matter are common knowledge.[4]

Committee members may and probably do, however, have *differing preferences*; some may be more concerned with inflation while others fret more about unemployment. Second, they might believe in *different models* of the economy. Such differences could be as minor as disagreeing over point estimates of the same parameters or as basic as holding entirely divergent conceptions of how the macroeconomy works. Third, committee members might make use of *different forecasts*, perhaps generated by various forecasting techniques.

Finally, there is an important dimension of difference that economists rarely think about. In our standard models, *Homo economicus* is an efficient calculating machine with no effective limits on the ability to handle huge amounts of data or to perform difficult computations.[5] But in real life, the implicit optimization problem facing a monetary policy committee is far too difficult to be solved explicitly. It may not even be tightly defined. So people bring different decision-making methods, sometimes called heuristics, to the table. They may therefore process the same information differently.

Having served for a time on the FOMC, I can assure you that committee members differed along all four of these dimensions. There were (and still are) "hawks" and "doves" whose relative preferences for low inflation versus high employment differed. There were (and are) monetarists and Keynesians and others with rather disparate models of how the economy works. The small number of people who have ever read the minutes or transcript of an FOMC meeting (Warning: These documents are not exactly John Grisham novels!) know that members often have differing views on where the economy is heading. And anyone who has ever grappled with a difficult decision in a group knows that individuals take different approaches to the same question—even in the presence of the same set of facts. To err is human, but humans err in an astonishing variety of ways.

So let's see what economic theorists have had to say about each of these four possible sources of differences inside a monetary policy committee.

*Different Preferences*

In principle, different personal judgments about, say, the relative social costs of inflation versus unemployment should be irrelevant— for a simple reason: The central bank's legal mandate should *tell* committee members what their loss function is, not *ask* them. So, for example, the British chancellor instructs the Bank of England to achieve 2.5 percent inflation within two years. An implicit loss function is buried within that edict. In principle, steering the economy then becomes a technocratic operation over which hawks and doves should not differ.[6]

Now contrast the crisply defined British objective function with the Fed's vague mandate to pursue both "stable prices" and "maximum employment." Neither goal is defined numerically; nor is anything said about how to deal with the short-run tradeoff. Congress's silence on these matters leaves a great deal of scope for FOMC members to interpret their legal mandate differently—and they do. So disputes at the Fed often pit hawks against doves—a fact that has not entirely escaped the attention of economic theorists (nor of the media!).

In one of the earliest contributions, Christopher Waller (1992) devised a model of how two political parties—think of one as more dovish, the other more hawkish—bargain over appointments to the MPC. Waller's focus was on how partisan the committee would be, and how that partisanship would change over the electoral cycle—not on why monetary policy is made by a committee. But his model contains an implicit answer to our central question: A committee structure with staggered terms of office creates checks and balances that moderate political influences on monetary policy.

Jon Faust (1996) also *assumed* that monetary policy was made by committee. He asked why the FOMC is such a strange amalgam of district bank presidents and politically appointed governors, and he answered that the peculiar voting structure was designed as a bulwark against inflation.[7] But Faust did not address a more basic question: If the concern is to make sure that the central bank is sufficiently hostile to inflation, why not just follow Rogoff's (1985) suggestion and appoint a single, conservative central banker? Paul Volcker acting alone will give you about as much anti-inflation zeal as you are likely to want.

Anne Sibert's (2001) model, a variant on the hawk–dove theme, is based on reputation. Having a reputation for inflation-aversion is helpful to a central bank because it holds down inflationary expectations. The key question for Sibert is how the *collective* reputation of an MPC is determined by the individual reputations of its members. Unfortunately, her main conclusion leaves us nowhere on our central question. In her model, either group or individual decision making could be superior on average, depending on the discount rate.

## Different Models

In the real world, different decision makers surely believe in different models of the economy. But as those of you familiar with the world of model building will understand, it is terribly difficult to build a tractable theoretical model around the simple insight that no one is quite sure what the right model is.

Petra Gerlach-Kristen (2001) has taken a small step in this direction by supposing that the macroeconomic models of the various MPC members differ in only one dimension: their estimate of potential output, $y^*$, which is of course very relevant to the outlook for inflation. Her answer to the question Why use committees rather than individuals? is both straightforward and reasonable. Each committee member receives a noisy signal of $y^*$. By pooling these estimates, a committee can derive an estimate of $y^*$ that is better than any individual's.[8] One clear implication of her model is that larger committees are better than smaller committees, which should give some comfort to the nineteen-member FOMC and the eighteen-member ECB Governing Council. Less obviously, Gerlach-Kristen (2001) shows that committees will be *less* inertial than individuals in adjusting interest rates. This is a highly counterintuitive result, and I will return to it below.

*Different Forecasts*

I do not know of any models of monetary policy based on the simple notion that members of the committee employ different forecasts. But Gerlach-Kristen's (2001) model can presumably be reinterpreted that way—after all, it is the *gap* between actual and potential GDP that drives inflation and therefore policy. Estimating y* high is a lot like estimating y low.

On the empirical side, there is intriguing evidence that predictions can be improved by combining a number of forecasts generated by different methods. For example, Armstrong (2001) surveys a number of studies covering a wide variety of applications and concludes that forecasting is normally improved by combining five or more *different* methods. It is just possible that MPCs perform such a function. Of course, one might argue that a single person with an open, flexible, and retentive mind—and a good staff—can combine many disparate forecasts as well as a committee can. But my strong guess is that several minds will perform this task better than one.

*Different "Optimization" Techniques*

Economists sometimes forget that our assumption that people solve incredibly complicated optimization problems is metaphoric, not literal. In reality, people cope with these problems as best they can— and in a wide variety of ways. In a fascinating theoretical paper, Lu Hong and Scott Page (1998) demonstrate that what they call diverse groups can outperform individuals or more homogeneous groups in solving complex problems. Their operational definition of *diversity* is that the members of the group employ different decision-making heuristics. Hong and Page (1998, 3) observe that this finding has "wide acceptance" among specialists in organizational behavior.

## Individuals versus Committees: Some Practical Considerations

So what lessons do we take away from this brief foray into theory? At least three reasons to prefer committees over individuals emerge. First, group decision making offers some insurance against the possibly extreme preferences of a dictatorial central banker—for example, one who might be obsessed with either low inflation or low unemployment. Second, the pooling of knowledge in an uncertain world should lead to better analysis and, therefore, to better decisions. Third, a group of people who process information and reach decisions differently may outperform even highly skilled individuals when it comes to the execution of complex tasks.

Each of these theoretical considerations rings true. Hawk–dove differences have already been mentioned. In principle, these should be irrelevant because the central bank's objective function should be given to it (perhaps implicitly) by the political authorities. In practice, they are not. And having a spectrum of opinion on a committee is one useful way to avoid extremes. There is also no doubt that members of the FOMC often reach diverse policy conclusions even though all of them see the same data. Some of these disagreements may stem from different loss functions. But others surely stem from different models, belief in different forecasts, and different ways of processing information. This is one case in which it strikes me that theorists have been barking up many of the right trees.

But is a committee necessary to reap these benefits of diversity? As hinted above, it is at least possible that a methodologically diverse central bank staff might capture many of the benefits for a *single* central bank governor. To some extent, this may happen now in real-world central banks. But the tendency toward group-think can be strong in an entrenched, self-confident bureaucracy. So I do not believe that a diverse staff is anywhere close to a perfect substitute for a diverse decision-making body.

Let me now add a few real-world considerations that have not figured prominently, if at all, in the theoretical literature.

It is sometimes claimed that group decision making is inherently more transparent than individual decision making—after all, it is hard to get inside a person's head. And I emphasized in chapter 1 that transparency has many advantages. So if there is a positive association between committee decision making and transparency, that would constitute a significant argument in favor of making monetary policy by committee. But is there such a correlation empirically? Are committees really more transparent?

The Bank of England and the Bank of Japan are often held up as examples: Both became vastly more open when they adopted formal monetary policy committee structures. But the Bank of Japan is still not a leader in terms of transparency, while more "dictatorial" central banks such as the Reserve Bank of New Zealand are. Similarly, the group decision-making processes at the FOMC and the ECBs Governing Council are far from models of transparency. So a casual look reveals no strong association between transparency and group decision making.

Is there any systematic empirical association? That is a difficult question to answer because neither transparency nor the nature of the central bank's decision making comes with any natural quantitative metrics. Look at figure 2.2. On the horizontal axis, I have ranked nine major central banks according to their degree of "democracy" in making monetary policy decisions—from the individual governor in New Zealand to the Bank of England's highly democratic MPC. This is an admittedly subjective ranking, but I checked it with several colleagues and made some modifications of my original views—an ersatz Delphi method. On the vertical axis, I have recorded the previously mentioned ranking for transparency created by Eijffinger and Geraats (2001) for these same nine central banks. Eyeballing this scatter plot suggests little correlation between transparency and group versus individual decision making. The computed rank correlation is just +0.11. In fact, for what it is worth, the diagram displays a distinct U-shaped pattern, with both the least democratic (New Zealand and Canada) and the most democratic central banks (the United Kingdom and Sweden) more transparent that the intermediate cases.

Thus the conclusion seems to be twofold. In principle, a single central bank governor can be extremely transparent if he chooses to be (or if the law directs him to be), and a committee can be opaque. In practice, there are cases of both.

But other arguments for committees may be more cogent. Consider the checks and balances argument mentioned earlier in the context of conflicts between hawks and doves. It can be generalized. For example, it is very difficult (though not impossible) for a sizable committee to be captured by an odd or highly idiosyncratic economic theory,[9] or even to adopt a forecast that is wildly at variance with the consensus. As I have said many times in the past, a little stodginess at the central bank is reassuring.

Speaking of stodginess, it is widely believed that groups are more inertial than individuals because, for example, of the need to build consensus. If true—and I will offer some surprising contradictory evidence shortly—that difference can be viewed either as a strength or a weakness of committee decision making. Remember that Newton's first law of motion comes in *two* parts. The first is that a body at rest tends to stay at rest. Analogously, an inertial MPC may need more provocation than an individual before it is moved to act. That sort of inertia creates a kind of buffer against excessively volatile policy, which can be beneficial. But it is also likely to make monetary policy slow off the mark. Second, however, Newton taught us that a body in motion tends to stay in motion—*in the same direction*. That

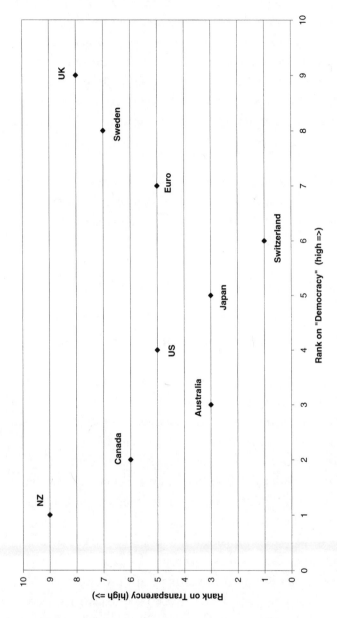

**Figure 2.2** Are More "Democratic" Central Banks More Transparent?

sort of inertia may be one reason central banks seem to make a habit of continuing to tighten or to ease for too long, thereby overshooting their targets.

Finally, the clean theoretical distinction between individual and group decision making is fuzzy in practice. With a few rare exceptions, central bank policy boards do not reach decisions by literal majority vote. Committees have chairmen, who may dominate the proceedings.

This fact is most obvious in the case of the Fed, where it is often believed—more or less correctly these days—that only one vote matters. On paper, the FOMC is a pure committee that reaches decisions by majority vote. In practice, each member other than Alan Greenspan has only one real choice when the roll is called: whether to go on record as supporting or opposing the chairman's recommendation, which will prevail in any case.[10] It is therefore quite possible for the Fed to adopt one policy even though the (unweighted) majority favors another.

Indeed, as unemployment fell and fell in the late 1990s, it was widely believed (and amply reported in the media) that the dovish chairman was holding back a more hawkish majority that wanted to raise rates. An even clearer example came in February 1994, when the Fed began a cycle of interest rate increases by moving the Federal funds rate up 25 basis points. The transcript of that meeting (which is now public) shows that a clear majority of the committee favored moving up by 50 basis points. Greenspan, however, insisted not just on 25 basis points, but on a unanimous vote for that decision. He got both.

This tradition of dominance by the chairman is probably stronger now than it has ever been, owing to Greenspan's long tenure on the job, his evident success, and his august reputation. But the tradition did not originate with Greenspan. Paul Volcker's dominance was also legendary. And a fascinating empirical study of

FOMC decisions under the chairmanship of Arthur Burns found that Burns's opinion counted roughly as much as all the rest of the committee members put together.[11] The authors did reject, however, the hypothesis that Burns in essence decided policy unilaterally. Empirically, the opinions of other FOMC members had some explanatory power for the committee's decisions.

## Do Committees Make Better Monetary Policy?

We have by now accumulated several reasons why a monetary policy committee might, in principle, be preferable to a single central bank governor making monetary policy alone. Briefly stated they are:

- Policy made by a committee is likely to be less volatile (more inertial).
- Committees are less likely than individuals to adopt extreme positions.
- A committee pools the knowledge of its members, which may be very useful in an uncertain world.
- Committee members bring different decision heuristics to the table, which can be very helpful in solving ill-defined or inordinately difficult problems.

Only the first of these might be turned around into an argument in favor of a single decision maker because inertia can be a curse as well as a blessing. The others point unequivocally toward committees. So, if we do not apply any weights to the preceding list, we are clearly left with more reasons to favor groups than individuals.

But there is a more important question: Do committees or individuals make better decisions? As a rough empirical generalization, psychologists have accumulated a significant, though not overwhelming, body of evidence that groups generally outperform individuals. An overly terse summary of the findings might be that groups normally do better than the average individual, but not by as large a margin as would be predicted by, say, a simple statistical model of pooling idiosyncratic knowledge.[12] There is also a suggestion in this literature that groups can be too large—presumably because of coordination problems.

Do these general findings apply to the specific context of making monetary policy? To get an idea, John Morgan and I (2004) conducted a laboratory experiment comparing hypothetical monetary policy decisions made by individuals and groups. I'd like to describe what we did,[13] both because the results were remarkable and because experimental methods are almost never applied to macroeconomic issues.[14]

Our experiment brought students into a computer laboratory in groups of five to simulate monetary policy making in an imaginary economy. Each student made monetary policy decisions for the same fictitious economy both as an individual and as part of a five-person committee.[15] Every play of the game lasted twenty periods, which subjects were told to think of as quarters. Thus one complete play of the game represented five years of macroeconomic history for an imaginary (but modestly realistic) economy.

Each computer in the lab was programed with the same simple two-equation macroeconomic model, which approximates models that have been used in the recent theoretical literature on monetary policy.[16] The precise model is given in the appendix to this chapter; here I will just describe its main features.

The models contains a standard accelerationist Phillips curve in which inflation, $\pi_t$, depends on lagged unemployment, $U_{t-1}$, and its own past history. This equation governs the model's long-run properties. But the real action is in the other equation, which relates this quarter's unemployment rate, $U_t$, to *current* fiscal policy and last period's monetary policy.

Fiscal policy is represented by government spending, $G_t$. (More on this variable shortly.) The effect of monetary policy on unemployment is represented by the *real* interest rate, $i_t - \pi_t$, where $i_t$ is the *nominal* interest rate. Just like actual Federal Reserve policy-makers, however, our experimental subjects could control only the nominal interest rate, not the *real* interest rate. In the model (as in reality), higher real interest rates push unemployment up, but only gradually, starting one quarter later. And lower real interest rates push unemployment down. Fiscal policy, which students do not control, also affects unemployment gradually; but its initial effects hit immediately. Because of the accelerationist Phillips curve, the model has an *equilibrium* unemployment rate, which is 5 percent. But students were not told that. They were, however, instructed to try to keep U as close to 5 percent as possible.

The fiscal shock, $G_t$, is the random variable to which our subjects were supposed to react. Students, who had to have some minimal understanding of macroeconomics in order to be admitted to the experiment, were told that G would either increase or decrease at a randomly selected time within the first ten quarters. It is clear enough from basic macroeconomics (and students were reminded, in case they had forgotten) that monetary policy should be adjusted to offset such a fiscal shock. If G rises (thus lowering unemploy-ment), monetary policy should be tightened by raising i. If G falls (thus raising unemployment), monetary policy should be eased by lowering i. But the trick is to know when to act—and by how much. Students were not told when G changed, nor by what amount, nor even in *what direction*. So they did not know exactly when or how to adjust the rate of interest—and perhaps not even in which direction.

You might think that this setup would pose an easy inference problem because, whenever G moves, unemployment moves in the opposite direction. But several other things are going on in the model at the same time. For example, each equation has a random shock, which adds pure statistical "noise" to the system. Further-more, lagged responses to prior events make the unemployment move around even when G is not changing. So the inference problem is far from trivial.

In brief, our experimental subjects had very little quantitative information about the structure of the model. They understood that, say, raising interest rates would reduce inflation and raise unemployment with a lag. But they did not know the magnitudes or timing of the responses. They knew that a fiscal shock would come along some time within the first ten quarters and that their principal task would be to offset it. But they were not told anything about the timing, size, or direction of the shock. Nor did they know any of the details of the model's specification, coefficients, or lag structure (all of which are displayed in the appendix to this chapter).

On the other hand, students were given a well-defined and easily understandable objective function, interpreted as a percentage score for each quarter. Specifically, subjects were told that they would be rewarded for keeping the unemployment rate as close to 5 percent and the inflation rate as close to 2 percent, as they could. Their score for each quarter started at 100 points, and they were penalized according to the absolute values of any deviations from target—losing 10 points for each full percentage point miss. So, for example, a 5.8 percent unemployment rate and a 1.4 percent inflation rate in a particular quarter would yield a score of $100 - 10(0.8) - 10(0.6) = 86$ for that quarter.

We ran twenty experimental sessions, each with five students. A session consisted of forty complete plays of the game, run in the following order: first ten as individuals, then ten in groups, then ten more as individuals, and finally ten more in groups. While the model was always the same, the sequences of random shocks were different in every play of the game. So each individual and every group experienced a somewhat different history each time they played the game.

Subjects were paid in cash at the end of the session, according to their overall average percentage scores, at the rate of $0.25 per percentage point.

Finally, we instituted a small charge of 10 points each time the interest rate was changed (no matter by how much) in order to deter excessive "fiddling" with monetary policy. Without this charge, we found (in trials of the game) that students would often move interest rates up and down quite a bit just to see what would happen. Averaged over a twenty-period game, each such 10-point penalty amounted to just 0.5 percent.[17] But that seemed to be enough to deter excessive experimentation.[18]

Because the *same* individuals made monetary policy decisions both as individuals and as members of a group, the experimental design created automatic controls for individual effects, that is, for systematic differences in ability from one subject to another. In the event, we found little statistical evidence that such differences existed. We also found little evidence of learning as the sessions progressed from the first play of the game to the fortieth—with one very important exception: Students' performance improved noticeably (and significantly) after their first experience with group play.

This last remark hints at our first main finding: On average, the groups outscored the individuals. Our twenty experimental sessions generated four hundred observations on group performance (twenty observations per session) and two thousand observations on individual performance (twenty observations per session for each of five students). The mean group score was 88.3 percent, while the mean individual score was only 85.3 percent. The difference is both highly significant statistically (t-ratio = 5.9) and large enough to be meaningful economically. One way to think about the latter is to look at it this way: The first interest rate change was made in the *wrong* direction 15.7 percent of the time in individual play, but only

9.5 percent of the time in group play. Thus group deliberations reduced this particular measure of the error rate by about 60 percent.

So that was our first main finding: Groups do better than individuals, on average. But what about speed of response, which also matters for monetary policy? The right policy taken a year too late may be the wrong policy.

As I mentioned earlier, nearly everyone on earth seems to believe that groups make decisions more slowly than individuals do. We believed that, too—before we did the experiments. Could it be that, even though the five-person committees changed monetary policy in the right direction more often than the individuals did, they reacted too slowly? If so, was that sluggishness such a severe handicap that it undermined the effectiveness of monetary policy as a stabilizer?

In our experiment, speed was measured by the number of periods that elapsed between the change in G and the subsequent response of monetary policy—that is, by how much information the decision makers required before taking action. Clock time was deemed to be irrelevant, and we did not measure it.[19] That omission was a deliberate choice, not a flaw in the experimental design. The experiment was designed to resemble actual monetary policy making as closely as possible. A real-life central bank board does not worry about how many minutes tick away while it is deliberating. Rather, it receives new data on the economy almost every day, and must decide when it has accumulated enough new information to warrant a change in policy.

Stunningly, our laboratory experiment did not support the commonsense view that groups are slower to react than individuals. The average lag of monetary policy behind changes in G was actually slightly *shorter* for the groups than for the individuals. But the small difference between the mean lag for groups (2.30 periods) and the mean lag for individuals (2.45 periods) was not statistically significant (t-ratio = 0.78). The basic conclusion is that the lags were roughly the same for individuals and for groups, which was our second main finding.[20]

To the extent that these experimental findings from the laboratory can be applied to the real world—and that is always a question—they suggest yet another reason to favor monetary policy making by committee: Groups make superior judgments without requiring more time to do so. If true, that may be the most powerful argument of all.

## What Kind of Committee?

In drawing the distinction between individual- and committee-based decision making, I have been too simplistic in at least one respect: Not all committees are created equal. FOMC decisions are widely believed to reflect Alan Greenspan's personal opinions, while Bank of England decisions are reached by a process that comes closer to pure majority voting. The FOMC reports its votes, while the ECB's Governing Council claims to reach consensus decisions without voting. The FOMC has nineteen members; the Swiss monetary policy committee has three. And so on.

Recognizing that variants exist, and that no two MPCs are exactly alike, I would nonetheless like to organize this discussion around the two stereotypes I introduced in the discussion of transparency in chapter 1. I call them "collegial" and "individualistic" committees. Many readers will recognize the two stereotypes as I describe them because you may have served on committees of each type in contexts other than monetary policy.

A *collegial committee* prizes solidarity and strives for group ownership of any decision that it makes. The chairman therefore tries to forge a strong consensus; the goal is unanimity, if humanly possible. He might achieve consensus by figuring out where the committee's center of gravity is and then pushing and cajoling the outliers to go along. Or he might try to impose his will on the committee, and then appeal for unanimity in the best interests of the organization.[21] But in either case, once a collegial committee reaches a decision, all of its members are expected to fall in line behind it. Voting is a formality—if, indeed, a vote is taken—for it is the group that is held accountable, not each member separately. Corporate boards of directors operate that way most of the time. Academic departments try to, not always successfully.

In an *individualistic committee,* by contrast, differences of opinion—where they exist—are of the essence, and little or no effort is made to suppress them. Members of the committee are expected to weigh the various pros and cons of alternative choices, argue them out, and then reach a conclusion by majority vote. There is no presumption that every member of the committee will then embrace the group's decision as if it was their own. Rather, individuals are expected to vote their personal preferences—and perhaps even to express those preferences publicly. Implicitly, each member is individually accountable for his or her own vote. Think of the U.S. Supreme Court as a model or, for that matter, a panel of Olympic figure-skating judges.

As I have already indicated, both species can be found in the real world of central banking (see fig. 2.3). At the collegial extreme, we find the ECB's Governing Council, which does not even take votes (or at least does not report them) and which staunchly maintains— to skeptical observers—that all of its decisions are unanimous. The FOMC is also a collegial committee in that it prizes consensus, seeks unanimity, and tries to speak with one voice. (In fact, while some critics say that it hardly speaks at all, others complain that it speaks with too many voices.) It is significant that the terminology used to describe a vote against the Fed chairman—a dissent—suggests some kind of abnormality.

**Figure 2.3**   Individualistic vs. Collegial Central Banks

At the opposite end, we find the highly individualistic monetary policy committees of the Bank of England and the Swedish Riksbank. While both committees are led by governors, both make monetary policy decisions by majority vote among (more or less) equal members. Opposing the governor is neither considered aberrant behavior nor viewed as a challenge to his authority.

There is also a broad middle ground. The Bank of Canada is one case in which it is debatable whether monetary policy is in fact made by a committee or by the governor acting alone. Putatively, it is a committee. But the committee lacks statutory authority and consists of the governor and his two top deputies. The Bank of Japan's policy board looks a bit more individualistic than the FOMC, but considerably less individualistic than the British MPC.

My question—the last one to be addressed in this chapter—is: Which type of committee structure is best suited to making monetary policy? If you were designing a central bank from scratch—as the European Union, the United Kingdom, and Japan all did in the 1990s—which sort of committee would you want to create?

*Individualistic Committees*

A truly individualistic committee reaches decisions in the same way that an idealized legislature makes laws—*not* in the way an actual legislature does. Positions are offered, the pros and cons are debated, committee members weigh the equities of the case, and then they vote. Think Athenian democracy—or at least the hagiographic version that we perceive through the purifying mists of history. (One suspects that the rank and file of ancient Athens saw things rather differently.)

The internal proceedings of an individualistic MPC may be quite messy because the group process thrives on, indeed requires, differences of opinion. It therefore must welcome internal disagreements and learn to manage them. Indeed, the potential strength of such a committee lies in the variety of different views and methods of analysis that its members can bring to bear on an issue. The individualistic structure also builds in strong safeguards against capture by an idiosyncratic theory, methodology, or ideology. Remember, for example, Waller's (1992) theoretical model, in which policy making by majority vote moderated partisanship because of staggered terms of office. That analysis points strongly toward individualistic committees in which members vote for their own preferred policies.[22]

Of course, such a freewheeling group may sometimes find it difficult to agree on what to do. We all know, for example, about the Arrow voting paradox.[23] More frequently, a highly individualistic committee will manage to reach a decision but then find it difficult to agree on the analysis and reasoning behind it—which can create a communication problem. A series of badly split votes may not inspire confidence that the central bank knows what it is doing, especially if the reasons for the disagreements are aired in public. Remember that one essential aspect of transparency is getting the markets (and the public, to the extent that it is interested) to think like the central bank. Accomplishing that may be extremely difficult if outside observers hear complicated weighings of pros and cons instead of coherent explanations of policy decisions. A central bank that speaks with a cacophony of voices may, in effect, have no voice at all.

So, for example, the very transparent but sometimes fractious Bank of England MPC finds it so difficult to agree on a postmeeting statement explaining its decision that it typically does not issue one.[24] On the other hand, when it is announced, the committee's vote conveys real information—in the way that the vote of a collegial committee does not.

## Collegial Committees

Which brings me to collegial committees. As I said earlier, they come in two varieties. In one type—the ECB Governing Council may be an example—the chairman seeks out and perhaps builds a consensus and then persuades recalcitrant members to go along. Call this a *genuinely collegial* committee. In the other type, the chairman's going-in position *is* the likely consensus, and he either persuades or browbeats the others into agreement. Call this an *autocratically collegial* committee. The latter is the FOMC model, except that nowadays Alan Greenspan's mythic stature is so intimidating that his opinion always prevails. Persuasion is almost automatic; all Greenspan needs to do is open his mouth.

The internal proceedings of a genuinely collegial committee may resemble those of an individualistic committee, including a vigorous but confidential internal debate. By contrast, the decision-making process of an autocratically collegial committee may be more like that of a single decision maker—in substance, if not in form. FOMC meetings, for example, are highly formal and polite affairs, very much controlled by the chairman. No one could realistically call them debates.

When it comes to policy making, however, the leader of even an autocratically collegial committee is still not in quite as dominant a position as a dictatorial central bank governor—precisely because of the aforementioned tradition of collegiality. The collegiality rubber hits the policy road in at least two prominent places.

First, if push ever comes to shove, the chairman knows that he lacks the de jure authority to force his committee members to accept his position. Rebellion is always possible, if the chairman is out of step with the committee. The strong desire for de facto consensus therefore enables the rest of the committee to serve as a kind of check on the chairman, who cannot easily pursue extreme policies, follow highly idiosyncratic procedures, or base policy on controversial theories.

Second, the desire to maintain the *appearance* of unity will sometimes force even a dominant chairman to tack in either the hawkish or dovish direction in order to keep wavering committee members on board. Alan Greenspan is about as dominant a chairman as you are ever likely to see. Yet even he occasionally modifies his position slightly (I emphasize the word *slightly*) in order to minimize dissent. He might do so by wording the statement in a way that placates some potential dissenters. Or he might do so by offering the so-called bias as a consolation prize to the losing side. (He might even allow the committee a "free vote" on the bias.) Or he might do so by shading his policy recommendation just enough to pick up a wavering voter or two. (Example: by moving the interest rate 25 basis points at the meeting instead of 50, with an idea to do the other 25 between meetings.) But whatever his chosen method, he leads the FOMC with a velvet glove, not with an iron fist.

When things are functioning smoothly, the communications you hear emanating from either type of collegial committee may sound alike—and they may be quite similar to what you would hear from a single decision maker. In particular, a collegial committee should be able to speak with one voice most of the time. Naturally, that will be easier for an autocratically collegial committee, where the chairman is the obvious spokesman, than for a genuinely collegial committee, where each member may feel entitled to express his or her nuance of difference. But even a nearly dictatorial chairman may find disaffected members sounding off in public if they feel that their views did not receive a fair hearing at the meeting. This has been known to cause problems for the FOMC on occasion.

*Toward an Optimal Committee*

So where do we come down in the end? Two main strands of argument point us in the direction of a monetary policy *committee* rather than a lone-wolf central banker. One is the economic and psychological evidence that committees, on average, outperform individuals in complex tasks. The other is diversification, broadly construed. We do not put all our financial eggs in one basket. Why, then, should we put all our monetary policy eggs in one basket? Compared to a single individual, a monetary policy committee seems to offer the well-known benefits of diversification: a higher mean with a lower variance.

Yet if the chairman is extremely dominant, an autocratically collegial committee may not diversify the nation's monetary policy portfolio much more than a single decision maker would. So the very lines of reasoning that favor committees over individuals appear to favor genuinely collegial committees or perhaps even individualistic committees over autocratic ones.

Wait, you might answer. Hasn't Alan Greenspan done a pretty superb job of leading the FOMC? Do you really want us to believe that a more egalitarian organizational structure at the Fed would have produced better results than benign dictatorship under Greenspan? No, I do not. The Greenspan record is remarkable. But it is also true that your portfolio would be worth a lot more today if you had invested it all in Microsoft twenty years ago instead of, say, buying the S&P 500. That fact does not, however, belie the wisdom of portfolio diversification. After all, you might have bet the ranch on Enron or WorldCom instead. We can identify the big winners only *ex post*, not *ex ante*—which is precisely why the first three rules of investing are diversify, diversify, diversify.

Similarly, putting all the national eggs in the Greenspan basket has served the country extremely well. But that was not so obvious when he was first appointed by President Reagan in 1987. And in the 1970s, we put all our eggs in the Arthur Burns basket—with rather less favorable results. The point is that picking a chairman of the Fed is a bit like investing your entire portfolio in a single stock. There is simply no guarantee that the nation will always, or even normally, hit the jackpot. Hence we are drawn back to the same simple principle: Diversify your central bank portfolio.

There is also a parallel political argument. Forgive me for saying so, but benign dictatorship is the most effective way to govern a large organization. It is certainly far more efficient than a messy, slow-moving, and highly political democracy, for example. Thus Yale and Princeton are run well as benign dictatorships. I shudder to think about how they would operate as true democracies. Fortunately, however, few political philosophers have seen fit to apply this "lesson" to the governance of nation-states, and for a very good reason: It is highly *risky* to rely on the kindness of dictators, who have a way of not remaining benign. Far better to take your chances with Madison's famous factions.

You may have noticed that, as I proceeded through the catalogue of reasons to prefer a monetary policy committee to a single individual, most of the reasons also pointed toward an individualistic committee structure, rather than an autocratic one. Except for one. A monetary policy committee that is too egalitarian runs a danger of speaking with too many voices. If the result is a cacophony rather than clarity, that may confuse rather than enlighten the markets and the public—thereby turning transparency into noise. And that, in turn, can hamper the operation of monetary policy.

Furthermore, the citizens of a democracy have a right to understand what their central bank is up to, *and why*. A bank that is incapable of explaining why it does what it does is failing to perform one vital aspect of its duty. Someone, presumably the chairman, must therefore speak definitively for the committee, or else somehow ensure that all the committee members sing from the same page. For that reason, too much democracy inside the central bank may not be such a good thing.

There should, in principle, be a kind of "interior maximum" where a monetary policy committee is individualistic enough to reap most of the benefits of diversity and yet collegial and disciplined enough to project a clear and transparent message. Such a committee might look fractious and argumentative from the inside, but united and like-minded from the outside. That is an elusive goal, to be sure, but it is one worth pursuing. And I believe it will take us in the direction of what I have called a genuinely collegial committee, albeit one with a clear leader.

## The Bottom Line

So what have we concluded in this chapter? First, there is an interesting fact: that modern central banks are moving away from the old norm of decision making by a lone individual toward a new norm of decision making by committee. As a matter of historical fact, this trend is probably due to the perceived success of the Fed and the Bundesbank, not to any grand new conceptual insights that you may have read here or elsewhere. But there are also several sound theoretical reasons, backed up by some supporting evidence, to favor a monetary policy committee over an individual governor.

Most of these reasons come down, in one way or another, to diversification of risk. A multimember committee pools preferences, models, forecasts, and much else—thereby reducing the risk that a dictatorial central bank governor might lead the bank astray. These same arguments would seem to favor individualistic committees over autocratically collegial ones, but you can carry individualism too far.

When the central bank's headquarters start to sound like the Tower of Babel, that's a sure sign that individualism has been carried too far.

## Appendix to Chapter 2: The Macroeconomic Model of Monetary Policy

The two-equation model used to assess the relative abilities of groups versus individuals to conduct monetary policy was as follows:

(2.1)     $\pi_t = 0.4\pi_{t-1} + 0.3\pi_{t-2} + 0.2\pi_{t-3} + 0.1\pi_{t-4} - 0.5(U_{t-1} - 5) + w_t.$

In this standard Phillips-curve equation, the weights on past inflation, which sum to one, can be thought of as representing expected inflation; but the model does not demand this interpretation. $U_t$ is the unemployment rate in quarter t, and the assumed "natural rate" of unemployment is 5 percent, as mentioned in the chapter. So U-5 is the deviation of unemployment from equilibrium. It affects inflation with a one-quarter lag. $w_t$ is a random inflation shock with standard deviation of 0.14.

The second equation generates the unemployment "gap" from its own lagged value, lagged monetary policy, and a fiscal shock:

(2.2)      $U_t - 5 = 0.6(U_{t-1} - 5) + 0.3(i_{t-1} - \pi_{t-1} - 5) - G_t + e_t$

Aficionados can think of it as a reduced form equation that combines an IS curve with Okun's Law. Since i is the nominal interest rate and $\pi$ is the rate of inflation, $i_t - \pi_t$ is the *real* interest rate, and the term $i_t - \pi_t - 5$ connotes the deviation of the real rate from its equilibrium, or "neutral," value, which happens also to be set at 5 percent.[25] Thus equation (2.2) says that higher (lower) real interest rates push unemployment up (down) but only gradually, starting one quarter later. The stochastic shock $e_t$ also has a standard deviation of 0.14. Since the standard deviations of the two stochastic shocks, $e_t$ and $w_t$, are about half the size of the G shock (which is

$\pm 0.3$), a change in G resembles a two standard deviation shock to e. Notice that the model is structured to make monetary policy affect inflation with a distributed lag that begins *two periods later*. A change in i affects U in the following period (see equation [2.2]), which in turn affects $\pi$ beginning a period after that (see equation [2.1]).

Finally, the objective function that students tried to maximize is

$$(2.3) \qquad score = 100 - 10\,|U_t - 5| - 10\,|\pi_t - 2|.$$

In words, subjects were supposed to keep the unemployment rate as close to 5 percent and the inflation rate as close to 2 percent, as they could. And they were penalized according to the absolute values of any deviations.[26]

# CHAPTER 3

# Following the Leader:
# The Central Bank and the Markets

Over the past decade or so, central bank independence has been the subject of a vast outpouring of academic literature,[1] a great deal of real-world debate in political and public policy circles, and a substantial amount of legal and institutional change in a wide variety of countries (not including the United States). Alex Cukierman (1998), who knows more about this subject than almost anyone else, has taken note of the strong worldwide trend toward greater central bank independence: Since 1989, more than two dozen countries have increased the independence of their central banks substantially. It seems that none have moved in the other direction. This trend has been widely applauded by economists, and for good reasons. Greater central bank independence appears to be associated statistically with superior macroeconomic performance,[2] although questions have been raised about the direction of causation.[3]

Just about 100 percent of this voluminous academic and real-world attention to central bank independence has been devoted to *independence from politics* and, in particular, from political influence over monetary policy. But there is another kind of independence that at least some strains of modern central banking may actually be endangering: *independence from the financial markets*.

What? you say. How can a central bank be independent of the markets when its policy actions work *through* markets, and when many of its most important indicators *are* market prices of one sort or another? Both objections are, of course, correct. When I speak of independence from the markets, I do not mean that central banks should either ignore market signals or rely on nonmarket methods for implementing monetary policy (for example, quantitative credit controls). What I *do* mean is that some modern central bankers seem to have become so deeply respectful of markets that a new danger is emerging: that monetary policymakers might be tempted to "follow the markets" slavishly, essentially delivering the monetary policy that the markets expect or demand.[4]

## Who's the Boss?

It was not always thus. If I may be forgiven for indulging in stereo-types for a moment, the older tradition viewed the central bank more as the stern schoolmarm disciplining the markets when they got out of line than as the eager and respectful student studying at the markets' knee. As both a positive and normative matter, there was little question about who was the leader and who was the fol-lower. Part of the central banker's job was believed to be surprising or even bullying the markets.

Attitudes today are radically different. Modern central bankers pay rapt attention to what markets think they are up to—often as embodied in futures prices that flash across the Bloomberg screen in real time. Normally, the bank is loathe to deviate from what the markets expect it to do. This is a two-way street, of course. Markets today scrutinize the central banks with an intensity once reserved for the Kremlin; and "don't fight the Fed" is a well-ingrained piece of Wall Street wisdom. But the point I want to make is that many more central bankers now than previously view the markets as repositories of great power and wisdom—as sages to be listened to rather than merely as forces to be reckoned with. As I will discuss later, there is one major exception to this new rule: When it comes to foreign exchange operations, central banks still strive to catch the markets off guard—even to push them around, if possible. But by and large, the evolving norm of behavior is just the opposite. Central banks often *listen* to the markets in both senses of that verb.

For the most part, this is a healthy development. Investors and traders do, after all, back up their beliefs with huge amounts of money—although skeptics will note that most of it is OPM (other people's money). Furthermore, as we economists are fond of pointing out, market prices succinctly summarize the collective wisdom of a vast number of people with diverse beliefs and access to different information. To believe that you can outwit the markets on a regular basis requires an extreme hubris that few if any modern central bankers have. Nor should they have it.

That said, I'd like to raise a question about whether the pendulum may perhaps have swung too far, whether the roles of leader and follower may have been reversed too sharply, whether what began as a healthy respect for markets may be in danger of devolving into worship of a false hero. In brief, whether the quiet revolution in modern central banking may have taken a good thing too far.[5]

I have one particular hazard in mind. Imagine a stereotypical monetary policy committee that scrutinizes the term structure of interest rates or the futures markets or both, observes what the markets expect it to do on a meeting-by-meeting basis, and then delivers precisely that policy. Such behavior may sound like the proper outcome of central bank transparency that I discussed and extolled in chapter 1. But it is actually something quite different. A fully transparent central bank keeps the markets well informed, teaches them about its way of thinking, and offers appropriate clues to its future behavior—thereby making the markets better predictors of the central banks' decisions. But in all these ways, the monetary authorities are *leading* the markets to what they see as the right conclusions. My concern is with a central bank that *follows* the markets rather than leads them.

On the surface, it might seem that following the markets should produce a pretty good policy record. After all, the resulting decisions would embody the aforementioned collective wisdom, which presumably far exceeds the combined wisdom represented on any monetary policy committee. But I fear that following the markets might lead to rather poor policy nonetheless—for several reasons.

One is that speculative markets tend to run in herds and to overreact to almost any stimulus,[6] whereas central bankers need to be cautious and to act prudently. I have often had occasion to cite *Blinder's Law of Speculative Markets*, which is based on a truly colossal amount of armchair empiricism. It is this: When they respond to news, the markets normally get the direction right but exaggerate the magnitude by a factor between three and ten. (*Three* connotes calm markets, *ten*, volatile ones.) Central banks, by contrast, must not get carried away. They should have the personality of Alan Greenspan, not of Jim Morrison.

I am aware that Bob Shiller's provocative original work on overreaction in the stock and bond markets (Shiller 1979, 1981) spawned a huge literature, some of which establishes that Shiller-like evidence may not actually demonstrate that markets typically overreact. There are alternative explanations of the data that are consistent with the efficient markets hypothesis. Maybe the daily dose of news absorbed by the stock market really *does* change the present discounted value of future dividends by about 1 percent—and by 23 percent on that fateful October day in 1987! (If you believe that, I have an efficiently priced dot.com I'd like to sell you.)

Much of this debate is highly technical, and this is neither the time nor the place to summarize, extend, or adjudicate it. Nor am I the person best qualified to do so. Let me just point out that Ptolemaic astronomy also had its ingenious defenders, whose cleverly constructed epicycles held back the Copernican tide for a while. As you can probably tell, I cast my vote with Shiller—as, by the way, do most market participants. As Fischer Black, who lived successfully in both worlds, once put it, markets look far more efficient from the banks of the Charles than from the banks of the Hudson.[7]

Taking it as a fact that financial markets frequently overreact, an interesting question is *why*. One presumptive explanation is herding behavior. Even people from Connecticut and New Jersey know *this* much about cattle and sheep: that while they may be individually rational, the behavior of the herd sometimes produces results that, shall we say, stray pretty far from group rationality. Just as lemmings follow their leaders over cliffs, the seventeenth-century Dutch placed their faith in tulip bulbs, and the early-eighteenth-century French followed John Law into oblivion. Lest we think that modern-day Americans are vastly more sophisticated than those simpletons of yore, it was not so very long ago that gullible investors scrambled to fork over literally unbelievable sums for shares of Internet companies that never had any realistic ideas about how to make money. (Remember the idea of "paying for eyeballs"?—that is, valuing companies on the number of website "hits" rather than on profits or even sales.)

There is by now a substantial theoretical and empirical literature on herding, most of which—having been produced by economists—pertains to what might be called *rational* herding, that is, cases in which A follows B for reasons that are perfectly (individually) rational.[8] For example, herding might be based on the belief that others have valuable private information. I learn that Warren Buffet has bought a stock, believe it is because he knows something I don't know, and therefore buy the stock myself. That may be quite rational. But if everyone emulates Buffet, the stock price may get pumped up way beyond anything that Buffet's private information (if he really has any) can plausibly justify. Other models of rational herding are based on the reputations of fund managers and the way they are compensated (for example, it may pay to stay with the pack). In such cases, rational behavior by individuals may (but need not) lead to inefficient market outcomes.

But models of rational behavior may not capture the most important reasons for the herding phenomenon we observe in real markets. For example, so-called momentum investing—which means buying a stock just because it has recently gone up—is plainly irrational by standard definitions because, in efficient markets, stock prices are supposed to approximate random walks. Thus a recent run-up in the price of a share per se offers no reason to believe that above-normal returns will accrue to those who buy in today. Yet the existence of a substantial amount of momentum investing is well known anecdotally and has been documented by several scholars.[9]

Detecting herding empirically is a daunting task for several reasons. First, there may be good "fundamental" reasons for everyone to rush for the exits—or for the entrances—at once, without having contracted the urge just by watching others. Think about Enron stock once the bad news became public in 2001. Or Argentina's slow-motion default in 2000–01. Or, on the upside, the reaction of a pharmaceutical company's stock to its announcement of a new blockbuster drug. Investors are not necessarily acting like a herd just because many of them do the same thing at the same time. Second, devising a measure of herding is no simple task.[10] Third, it may be next to impossible to distinguish between rational and irrational herding. On the other hand, this last distinction may not be too important for present purposes since either type of herding behavior can lead to overreaction in markets—the phenomenon that concerns us here.

Although I have dwelt on it, herding behavior is just one of several possible explanations for systematic overreaction in speculative markets. Another, related explanation is that financial market participants frequently succumb to fads and fancies, producing speculative bubbles that may diverge sharply from fundamentals.[11] If learning that buying shares of stupid-idea.com is the in thing to do makes you too long for shares in the company, then the market may display positive feedback loops that produce more volatility than the fundamentals can justify. But central bankers must steadfastly resist such whimsy and inoculate themselves against the faddish behavior that so often dominates markets. That may be why central bankers are not much fun at parties.

Last, but certainly not least, there is the nasty matter of time horizons. *Homo economicus* has a long (perhaps infinite) time horizon and a reasonable discount rate. So, I hope, do most central bankers. But traders in real-world financial markets seem to have neither. One might hope that Darwinian mechanisms would select for patient, long-term investors—but they do not appear to do so in markets that are dominated by daily mark-to-market, quarterly reporting, and compensation based on short-term performance.

Here is a stunning quantitative example that I have cited before.[12] According to the standard theory of the term structure of interest rates, about which I will have critical things to say shortly, the thirty-year bond rate should be the appropriate average of the one-year bill rates that are expected to prevail over each of the next thirty years. Only one of these, today's one-year rate, is currently observed in the market. But the others—the so-called *implied forward rates*—can be inferred from the term structure. I will explain this in more detail shortly. But, for now, a simple example will do.

Suppose today's observed one-year interest rate is 3 percent and the two-year rate is 4 percent. Together, these imply that the one-year rate expected to prevail one year from now must be about 5 percent. The reason is straightforward. Investing in the two-year bond will leave you with $(1.04)^2$ two years later, after compounding. On the other hand, investing in two consecutive one-year bonds will be expected to earn you $(1.03)(1+r)$, where r is the one-year rate expected to prevail a year from today. Since arbitrage dictates that the two returns must be more or less equal, r must be approximately 5 percent.[13] Proceeding similarly, one can use the term structure to deduce all the implied forward rates, as I will demonstrate shortly. But now back to the time horizon issue.

One day in 1995, while serving as vice chairman of the Federal Reserve Board, I was wondering about bond market overreaction—which I thought I was witnessing all around me. So I asked the Fed staff to do a calculation. What, I inquired, is the correlation between *daily changes* in the one-year interest rate on U.S. Treasuries and *daily changes* in the implied one-year forward rate expected to prevail twenty-nine years from now? I was pretty sure I knew the theoretically correct answer to this question: essentially zero, because hardly any of the news that moves interest rates on a daily basis carries significant implications for interest rates twenty-nine years in the future. Modern-day Ptolemaists will, of course, insist that I am wrong about this. They will argue that things often happen that should have similar effects on both current interest rates and rates twenty-nine years from now. Oh? Name two.[14]

In any case, the statistical answer for the year 1994 was +0.54.[15] Taken literally, this correlation means that you can explain 29 percent of the variance of changes in the one-year interest rate 10,585 days from now by using nothing but today's change. Don't bet Yale's endowment, or even your own, on that!

So why is the correlation so high? My hunch, which I will develop in greater detail shortly, is that it reflects overreaction stemming from excessively short time horizons. The men and women who traded the thirty-year bond in 1994 (like the folks who do it today) were probably not thinking about the implications of various bits of news for the economy in the year 2024. Indeed, many of them probably had a hard time getting their arms around the concept of thirty years, having not yet attained that august age themselves. Instead, I believe, traders were buying and selling the long bond as if it were a much shorter instrument.

If this hunch—and I admit that it is no more than that—is correct, there is a supreme irony here. One of the chief arguments for making central banks *politically* independent is that monetary policy requires a long time horizon, not the notoriously short time horizons of elected politicians. But if the central bank follows the market too slavishly, it will tacitly and inadvertently adopt the market's short time horizon as its own. Politicians may focus on the next election, which is bad enough. But bond traders may focus on their positions at the end of the trading day, or perhaps a half-hour from now, which is much worse. A politically independent central bank that follows the whims of the markets may thus wind up with an effective time horizon even shorter than that of a politician.

It is also very likely to overreact, just as the markets frequently do. Here is a simple example. Suppose something happens that should, on rational grounds, induce the central bank to raise interest rates, but only very slightly—say, by 25 basis points. Perhaps the government issues a bad-looking inflation report for a single month, or something like that. The market sees this new information but exaggerates its significance. It therefore begins to embody expectations of, say, a 75-basis-point rate hike into asset prices. The central bank reads the market's expectations from the term structure and feels compelled to deliver something closer to what the market expects, say, 50 basis points, rather than "disappoint the markets." In this instance, the central bank's reaction is twice as large as it should be. While this is an exaggerated example, it serves to make the general point: If markets overreact and central banks follow the markets, then central banks are likely to overreact, too.

More analytically, my Princeton colleagues Ben Bernanke (who is now a Fed governor) and Michael Woodford (1997) have built a rational expectations model in which a central bank can create a multiplicity of equilibria by reacting to *the market's* forecast of inflation rather than to its own. They emphasize the importance of the central bank using *its own* inflation forecast rather than relying on the market's, which, in the context of their model, is the only way the bank can maintain its independence from the market.

## A Case in Point: The Term Structure of Interest Rates

I just used the term structure of interest rates to illustrate the general phenomenon of overreaction. This was no idle choice. In fact, one does not get very far in discussing central banking practice without mentioning the term structure. The so-called *expectations theory of the term structure*, to which I alluded earlier, is the vehicle almost always used to assess what the markets expect the central bank to do. It is therefore critical to communication between the central bank and the markets—in both directions. The question I want to deal with next is whether the markets are communicating well-considered wisdom to the central bankers or something rather less valuable. If the latter, of course, the central bank should listen rather selectively.

The role of the term structure is also central to the *transmission mechanism* of monetary policy, and for a very simple reason. Monetary policymakers generally have direct control over only the overnight interest rate. In the United States, that is the federal funds rate, the interest rate at which some banks lend reserves to others. At any one time, only a small minority of banks is active in this market. More fundamentally, as I noted earlier, no economic transaction of any importance takes place at the federal funds rate. If the Fed's monetary policy is to succeed in influencing the interest rates and asset prices that really matter—such as loan rates, bond rates, exchange rates, and stock market valuations—then changes in the funds rate must somehow be transmitted to these other financial variables. The expectations theory of the term structure provides the standard linkage.

The theory itself starts with a simple arbitrage argument. As in the numerical example above, an investor can buy a two-period bond and hold it to maturity or buy a one-period bond and roll it over into another one-period bond when the first one matures. If each strategy has adherents, the expected returns on the two strategies must be equal. That means that, roughly,[16] the two-period interest rate must be equal to the average of the two one-period rates—the first of which is actually observed in the marketplace today and the second of which is an (implicit) expectation. Using obvious symbols,[17]

(3.1) $$r_{2,t} = (1/2)(r_{1,t} + r^e_{1,t+1}),$$

where $r_{1,t}$ and $r_{2,t}$ are, respectively, the one- and two-period interest rates prevailing at time t, and the superscript e indicates an *expectation*. In this case, $r^e_{1,t+1}$ is the one-period rate expected to prevail one period from now. In the simple numerical example, the two-year rate was 4 percent, the one year rate was 3 percent, and we deduced that the one-year rate expected to prevail one year from now had to be 5 percent because 4% = ½(3% + 5%). Note that this relationship should hold whether time is measured in days, weeks, months, or years.

Similar relationships hold for three-period interest rates, four-period interest rates, and so on. Thus $r_{1,t}$, $r_{2,t}$, $r_{3,t}$ and so on—the constituent parts of what is called "the yield curve"[18]—depend crucially on *expectations*. If you think of time as measured in days, it is clear that the entire term structure should, in principle, be driven by expectations of what future monetary policy will be. For example, the one-*year* interest rate should embody today's one-*day* rate and the next 364 *expected* one-day rates; the ten-year interest rate should embody the next 3,649 expected one-day rates (forgetting about leap years); and so on.

As we move out along the yield curve to longer maturities, a term premium—variously rationalized as a *risk* premium or a *liquidity* premium—is generally added to the right-hand sides of equations like (3.1) to represent what investors demand to be paid to compensate them for the higher risk or lower liquidity of longer-dated instruments. In practice, the use of these premiums sometimes borders on the tautological: If the two sides of an equation like (3.1) appear to move differently, you can always square the circle with the appropriate time-varying risk premium. But the main point for present purposes is that interest rates on medium- and long-term debt instruments should depend mainly on expectations of future central bank policy.

This little detour into term structure theory explains why expectations are so central to the monetary policy transmission mechanism. A Federal Reserve action that strongly affects expectations of future short-term interest rates will, according to the theory, have a much greater impact on long-term interest rates than an action that moves today's short rate but leaves expected future short rates largely unaffected.

Equations like (3.1) can be used to deduce the expected future short rates (called implied forward rates) that I mentioned before. For example, it follows immediately from equation (3.1) that

(3.2) $$r^e_{1,t+1} = 2r_{2,t} - r_{1,t} .$$

The logic behind (3.2) is straightforward. If you earn the two-year rate for two years, you get (approximately) $2r_{2,t}$. If you earn the one-year rate for one year, you get $r_{1,t}$ . Equation (3.2) then answers the question How much must investors be expecting to earn in the second year?

More complicated versions of (3.2) will produce any implied forward rate you want. For example, I will shortly look at the *nine-year-ahead* forecasts of the *one-year* interest rate, in which case:

$$(3.3) \qquad\qquad r^e_{1,t+9} = 10r_{10,t} - 9r_{9,t} \, .$$

In words, if a prospective investor can earn $r_{10,t}$ annually for ten years with one strategy and $r_{9,t}$ annually for nine years with the other strategy, then she must be expecting to earn $10r_{10,t} - 9r_{9,t}$ in the remaining year. Since everything on the right-hand sides of equations like (3.2) and (3.3) can be observed directly in the market, the implied forward rates are easily computed, and financial specialists do so routinely.[19]

So far, so good. But here's the rub. The implied interest rate forecasts (expectations) that can be deduced from the yield curve bear little resemblance to what future interest rates actually turn out to be. There is no space here—and probably even less patience among readers—for a thorough review of the empirical evidence on the term structure of interest rates.[20] Suffice it to say that the abject empirical failure of the expectations theory of the term structure of interest rates is a well-established fact.

I will offer just two kinds of simple evidence here. The first is for ordinary people—simple pictures. The second is designed for professionals—simple regressions. Both derive from the same sort of equation—versions of (3.2) and (3.3).

Look first at figure 3.1, which offers a kind of eyeball test of equation (3.3). The right-hand side of (3.3), which is observable every day in the market, is a *forecast* of the one-year rate expected to prevail nine years from today. We can assess the accuracy of such forecasts historically by comparing them to the one-year interest rates that actually obtained nine years later, provided we are willing

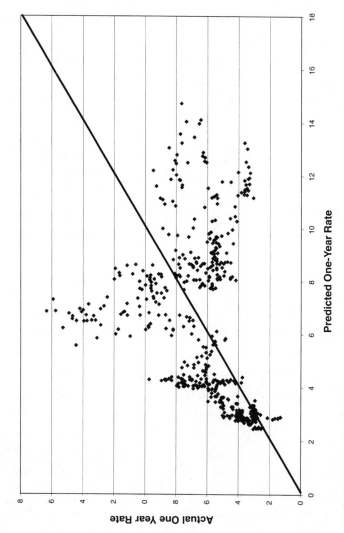

**Figure 3.1** Predicted vs. Actual One-Year Interest Rates

to wait nine years. Figure 3.1 does precisely this, using monthly data on the yields on zero-coupon bonds over the period December 1949 to February 1991.[21]

On the horizontal axis, I plot the *forecasted* one-year bond rate nine years (that is, 108 months) later, computed from equation (3.3) for each month in the sample period. On the vertical axis, I plot the *actual* one-year rate 108 months later. In principle, the two should be equal, except for random forecasting errors. The straight line shown in the graph is *not* the best-fitting regression line, but rather a line with a slope of one—indicating the theoretically correct relationship.[22] You do not need advanced training in statistics to see that the forecasts are pretty terrible. In fact, there appears to be little relationship between the two variables.

For those who do have such training, I offer two regressions. The first regresses the actual interest rate, $r_{1,t+9}$, on the forecast, $r^e_{1,t+9}$, as defined by equation (3.3), and tests the restriction that the slope coefficient is 1.0. Unsurprisingly given the picture, the null hypothesis is easily rejected. In fact, the resulting point estimate of the slope is just 0.27 (with standard error 0.037).[23] The second comes from the existing literature—in particular, from a paper by John Campbell (1995, 139). It uses a variant of the term structure logic in which this month's yields on one-month and twelve-month zero-coupon bonds are used to forecast how the one-month yield should change over the ensuing eleven months.[24] Once again, his equation has the feature that the estimated slope parameter would be 1.0 under the expectations theory. But his estimate is only 0.25 with standard error 0.21. That point estimate, which is quite close to mine, is significantly different from the theoretically correct value of 1.0 but not significantly different from zero.

In brief, what we seem to have found is that the expectations theory of the term structure performs miserably over moderate (one-year) and long (ten-year) time horizons.[25] The empirical failure of the expectations theory of the term structure raises an obviously interesting question: Why? Why does a theory that seems so obviously correct in principle work so poorly in practice?

There is another, equally fascinating question, however. The theory's abject failure is not some deep, dark secret that we professors know about but have somehow kept from the rest of the world. Central bankers realize that the expectations theory does not work. So do market participants, who nonetheless appear to use it to guide billion-dollar interest rate bets each day. Yet, in what appears to be a stunning example of pretending that the emperor is still fully dressed, academic economists, central bankers, and market participants alike all proceed as if the expectations theory really underpins the term structure. It's a curious case of mutually agreed self-delusion, and the question is how and why it persists.

Freed, as I am in this book, from the heavy burden of peer review, I would like to suggest tentative answers to each of these questions.

First, why do experts continue to use the expectations theory of the term structure despite overwhelming evidence against it? My answer is that doing so is an act of desperation—they have no alternative. On a priori grounds, it is hard to understand how the expectations theory could be wrong. If expectations of future short rates do not determine long rates, then what does? I must admit that I have a hard time answering that question myself, and so I frequently find myself using the expectations theory to interpret the yield curve anyway. It's a bad habit that is hard to kick. Rarely has the old saw "it takes a theory to beat a theory" been leaned on so hard.

Second, why does the theory fail so miserably in explaining the facts? That may be the harder question. It is also the one most relevant to thinking through what the central bank can (or cannot) learn from the yield curve. I want to offer two candidate answers, while leaving the ultimate resolution of the issue, as usual, to the proverbial subsequent research. The two answers are consistent with one another. Each denies that expectations are rational. And each explains why the implied forward rates—the *expectations*—are overly sensitive to current rates, and therefore why long rates overreact to short rates.

My first candidate answer, which I offer with some trepidation and only because both New Haven and Princeton are so far from the Great Lakes, was suggested earlier; but let me repeat it now. I believe that, when it comes to pricing long-term bonds, market participants do not peer as far into the future as the theory says they should. Instead, they are systematically myopic and extrapolative, treating and trading longer-term instruments as if they were much shorter-dated instruments. One consequence is that the current situation and the latest news get far too much weight in setting today's long-term interest rates.

If this is so, then the amazingly high correlation between the one-year interest rate and the implied forward rate twenty-nine years from now becomes understandable. If traders treat the thirty-year bond as if it were, say, a three-year bond, then it is not hard to see why its price should respond strongly to short-term influences. Generalizing this example, we see that artificially short time horizons offer a straightforward explanation of Shiller's (1979) evidence for the overreaction of long rates to short rates.

The second explanation dispenses with rational expectations in a different way. A long-neglected paper by my Princeton colleague Gregory Chow, published in 1989, starts with the usual finding: The data he studies resoundingly reject the joint hypothesis that the expectations theory of the term structure holds *and* that expectations are (statistically) rational.[26] Furthermore, the estimated parameters make no sense. Chow (1989) then inquires into which is the weak sister. His answer is clear. When he replaces the assumption of rational expectations with *adaptive* expectations, he finds that the estimated parameters in the term structure equation are reasonable and that the joint hypothesis is *not* rejected. In other words, the expectations theory fails under rational expectations but works just fine under adaptive expectations.

Interesting. But how does that relate to the short-time-horizons idea? Simple. It turns out empirically that, compared to rational expectations, adaptive expectations place much greater weight on current short rates. In Chow's estimated example, under rational expectations a sustained 100-basis-point increase in the one-month rate has no effect on the twenty-year rate in the same month, only an 11-basis-point effect after three months, and only a 21-basis-point effect after six months.[27] But under adaptive expectations, the contemporaneous reaction is 20 basis points, the three-month reaction is 33 basis points, and the six-month reaction is 45 basis points.[28]

In sum, relative to rational expectations, both adaptive expectations and, I would suggest, actual human behavior put far too much weight on current market conditions. This finding will not surprise anyone who has not been unduly influenced by advanced training in economics. And if it is true, delivering the monetary policy that is expected, if not indeed demanded, by the (myopic) markets could lead a too-compliant central bank down a primrose path. So this is one case—and an important case at that—in which it is important that the central bank not take its lead from the markets.[29]

## Another Case in Point: Uncovered Interest Rate Parity

An analogous problem with interpreting market signals—and imbuing them with too much wisdom—arises in an international context. Instead of thinking about the arbitrage-like relations that arise in choosing among instruments of different *maturities*, as we do in the term structure, now think about choosing among instruments denominated in different *currencies* (over the same maturity). To start once again with a simple concrete example, suppose one-year U.S. Treasury bills are paying 4 percent *in dollars* at a time when equally-safe one-year German government bills are paying 3 percent *in euro*. The theory of *uncovered interest rate parity* is based on the following simple but compelling insight: If some investors choose the U.S. paper while others choose the German, then the two must have (approximately) equal *expected* yields—whether you measure that yield in dollars or in euro. For that to be the case, the euro must be expected to *appreciate* by 1 percent over the year relative to the dollar.

Let's be more precise. If you invest $100 in the U.S. paper, you will get back $104 at the end of the year, with certainty. Alternatively, you can (a) purchase 100 euros (using an exchange rate of $1 = 1 euro, and ignoring commissions), (b) invest that money at 3 percent to get back 103 euro after a year, and then (c) convert those euro into dollars at whatever exchange rate, X, then prevails. Doing all this will earn you 103/X *dollars*. A simple arbitrage-like argument says that, with risk-neutral investors, these two investment strategies must offer the same expected return—which is the basic insight underlying uncovered interest parity. In the specific example, $103/X^e$ must be approximately equal to $104, so that $X^e$ must be 0.9904.[30] Thus, for the 4 percent U.S. interest rate and the 3 percent German interest rate to coexist in financial market equilibrium, the euro must be expected to appreciate from $1 per euro to $1/0.9904=$1.0097 per euro, or by approximately 1 percent.

Generalizing this simple example, uncovered interest rate parity states that, for two equally risky instruments denominated in different currencies but covering the same time period (any time period will do):

$$(3.4) \qquad r^d = r^f + x^e,$$

where $r^d$ is the domestic-currency interest rate, $r^f$ is the foreign-currency interest rate, and $x^e$ is the expected rate of appreciation of the foreign currency. ($x^e$ is negative if the foreign currency is expected to depreciate.) Equations like (3.4) tie interest rates and exchange rate expectations tightly together. The age-old question is, Which moves which?

To see why this question is relevant to monetary policy, let's consider an application that is near and dear to the hearts of central bankers. Think of $r^d$ and $r^f$ as very short term interest rates, more or less controlled by the Fed and the ECB, respectively. Now suppose the Fed raises $r^d$, but the ECB does not change $r^f$. By the logic underlying (3.4), the expected change in the exchange rate must adjust upward. Specifically, the euro must now be expected to *appreciate more* or *depreciate less* than was the case just prior to the Fed's move. If the exchange rate expected to prevail a year from now is not changed by this event, as theoretical models generally assume, that means the dollar must *rise now* in order to create the expectation that it will *fall later*. On the other side of the Atlantic, of course, the ECB may be less than thrilled by the immediate depreciation of the euro. But, according to the logic behind equation (3.4), there is not much it can do about it—short of raising its domestic interest rate to match the Fed's. Like it or not, uncovered interest parity puts central banks in bed with one another. This is one-worldism in the extreme.

Now to the bad news. Think of equation (3.4) as a way to forecast changes in the exchange rate. It says, for example, that the expected rate of appreciation of the euro must be equal to the interest rate differential.[31] Thus, by examining interest rates here and abroad, you can read an implicit forecast of where exchange rates are expected to go from market prices—just as interest rates on short- and long-term debt imply a forecast of where short rates are expected to go. Thus, equation (3.4) is a market-based forecasting equation, similar in spirit to equation (3.2). Having read that, you can probably guess the punch line. Yes, the exchange rate forecasts implied by uncovered interest rate parity are truly terrible.[32] Don't bet a nickel on them.

Once again, there is a substantial scholarly literature on this point. And, once again, I'll gloss over this literature and offer just two pieces of supporting information. The first is a pair of simple graphs comparing the *forecasts* of exchange rate changes based on interest rate differentials to the exchange rate changes that *actually* occurred. Figures 3.2 and 3.3 both use data on the dollar/yen exchange rate and interest rate data on government debt in Japan and the United States. In figure 3.2, I compare the actual *three-month* change in the exchange rate to the forecast implied by three-month Treasury bill rates in the two countries three months earlier. Not only is the relationship not tight, it is actually perverse: Amazingly, the yen typically *de*preciated when its short-term interest rate was below the U.S. rate. Figure 3.3 compares *ten-year* exchange rate forecasts derived from equation (3.4) with actual realizations. There appears to be virtually no relationship between the two.

For readers who are regression-minded, notice that (3.4) suggests the following linear regression:

$$(3.5) \qquad x = a + bx^e + e = a + b(r^d - r^f) + e.$$

A regression fitted to the data underlying figure 3.2 has a slope coefficient of *minus* 3.3 (with a Newey-West standard error of 0.79), whereas the theoretically correct coefficient is 1.0. Surprisingly, the best fitting regression for figure 3.3 has a slope of 1.04 (standard error 0.22)—so, of course, we cannot reject b = 1. But a glance at figure 3.3 reminds us that the interest rate differential has a terrible forecasting record.

This finding is not special to the dollar/yen exchange rate or to the time horizons I have selected. Shusil Wadhwani (1999), while a member of the Bank of England's Monetary Policy Committee, called attention to the failure of uncovered interest parity by running regressions similar to (3.5) for several different exchange rates over a one-year horizon. Not only are his estimates of b not equal to

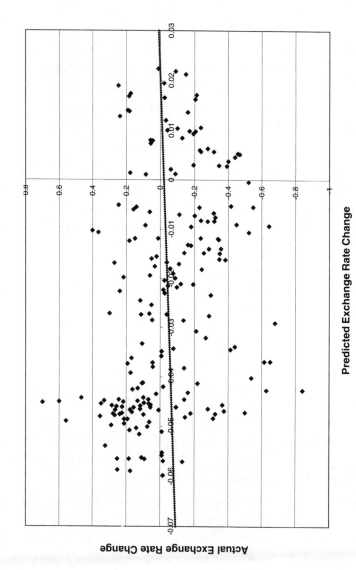

**Figure 3.2** Predicted vs. Actual Exchange Rate Changes over Three Months

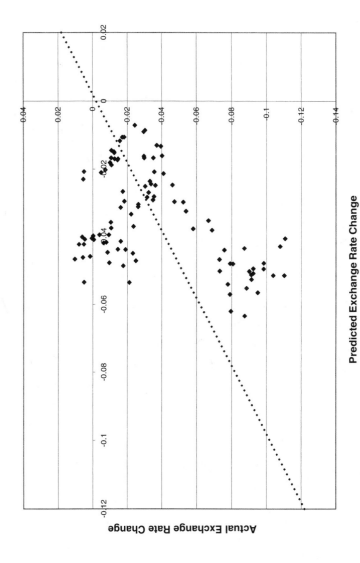

**Figure 3.3** Predicted vs. Actual Exchange Rate Changes over Ten Years

+1.0, they are actually all *negative*.[33] Never mind accuracy. This means that interest rate differentials actually would have pointed you in the wrong direction, just as indicated by figure 3.2.

So once again we have a major intellectual puzzle: A theory with seemingly impeccable logical credentials fails miserably in empirical tests. Interest rate differentials turn out to be horrible forecasters of changes in exchange rates. In fact, random walk models—which simply assume that exchange rates will never change—make better forecasts. Economists have been aware of this annoying fact ever since Meese and Rogoff's (1983) important paper. But they have yet to explain it.

So let me speculate about reasons. Once again, short time horizons and extrapolative behavior by traders probably play major roles, in stark contrast to the assumptions of rational expectations models. For example, more than twenty years ago, studies of the profitability of trading on exchange rate forecasts from three different sources—chartists, services based on "fundamentals," and forward exchange rates—found that the chartists' forecasts did best and the fundamentals-based services did worst.[34] I must say that this corresponds to my own casual observations of markets—they appear to be extrapolative in the short run. Note that since chartists base their predictions solely on recent price movements, *any* evidence of profitable trading based on chartist analysis represents a clear refutation of market efficiency—just as momentum trading does for stocks.

It is, furthermore, fascinating to note that the failure of uncovered interest parity is much more spectacular at short time horizons—where trading based on extrapolative expectations may dominate—than it is at long time horizons. This finding is consistent with our two graphs, which showed much worse performance of uncovered interest parity over three months than over ten years. It is also consistent with the scholarly literature.[35]

From a central banker's point of view, the routine violation of uncovered interest parity at short horizons creates a serious problem. Suppose you are the Fed, thinking about cutting interest rates ($r^d$ in equation [3.4]) and wondering what impact this action will have on the economy. One of the standard channels of monetary transmission is, of course, through the exchange rate. So one of the things you are wondering about is how your action will affect the value of the dollar. If you believe that the other major central banks will *not* match your rate cut, equation (3.4) says that reducing the federal funds rate will make the dollar *fall* first in order to create expectations of a subsequent *appreciation*. A cheaper dollar should help U.S. exports and discourage U.S. imports, thereby boosting aggregate demand and giving your monetary policy an assist. But as a well-educated central banker, you are also aware that exchange rate forecasts generated by uncovered interest parity are terribly inaccurate. So you have little confidence that any of this will actually happen. How, then, do you reckon the exchange rate channel into your calculations?

In practice, this intellectual puzzle seems to have deepened in recent years. The new conventional wisdom is that boosting the economy by cutting interest rates may actually make the currency *appreciate* immediately, presumably because a stronger macroeconomy improves prospects for (mostly financial) investment and attracts larger capital inflows. Notice that this new "model" of how the exchange rate reacts to monetary policy is precisely the opposite of what the textbooks teach.[36] I was brought up to believe that easier money made your currency *depreciate*. (Of course, in those days we also walked barefoot over glass to get to school—uphill in both directions.) Nowadays, what I used to deride as the "macho theory of exchange rates"—the idea that the exchange rate reflects the nation's virility—is looking better and better.

I hasten to say that the macho theory is now the market's belief only for major countries like the United States, Europe, and Japan. No one to my knowledge has suggested it for Argentina or Turkey. Yet recent evidence questions even the standard view that emerging-market countries can defend their exchange rates by jacking up interest rates. They may just kill their economies instead.[37]

## The Special Case of Foreign Exchange Intervention

Up to now, I have been speaking about central bank operations that are designed to change interest rates—which, of course, is what we generally mean by monetary policy. Exchange rate movements were only a by-product, although perhaps an important one. But sometimes a central bank—either on its own authority or under orders from the Treasury or Finance Ministry—intervenes in the foreign exchange market with the expressed intent of changing the (otherwise floating) exchange rate without changing the domestic interest rate.[38] Economists call such operations *sterilized interventions* because they insulate domestic monetary conditions from exchange rate intervention.[39] The question is, Can sterilized foreign exchange interventions work?

To someone who has not studied economics beyond the 101 level, the answer may seem self-evident. If the Fed enters the market to sell dollars, the dollar falls. If it buys dollars, the dollar rises. Right? Well, maybe not. Remember equation (3.4) again. In a sterilized intervention, $r^d$ does not change—under the assumption that domestic and foreign assets are *perfect substitutes*. Presumably, $r^f$ doesn't either. In that case, $x^e$ should not change, and so neither should the exchange rate.[40]

To readers unfamiliar with such arguments, this may seem a bit like pulling a rabbit out of a hat. So here is an analogy for noneconomists. Suppose Coke and Pepsi are perfect substitutes in the eyes of consumers. That means that, at equal prices, they do not care which one they drink—but if the price of either soft drink rises by even a penny, customers will move *en masse* to the other drink. Now suppose the government tries to drive up the price of Pepsi (and drive down the price of Coke) by offering to buy Pepsi and sell Coke. Can this intervention possibly succeed? Not under the hypothesis of perfect substitutability, for then even the slightest price advantage for Coke will give virtually the entire market to Coca-Cola. So the two prices cannot differ, except fleetingly. If the government sells Coke to buy Pepsi, private parties will do just the reverse. The prices must remain equal.

Perfect substitutability works in the same way to negate the effects of a sterilized foreign currency intervention. The central bank, for example, *buys* domestic Treasury bills and *sells* foreign Treasury bills of equal market value. In principle, that should lower the domestic interest rate and raise the foreign interest rate. But if foreign and domestic bills are perfect substitutes in the eyes of investors, private investors will willingly sell as much of the domestic issue as the government offers to buy and buy as much of the foreign issue as the government offers to sell—all with virtually no change in any price. Neither $r^d$ nor $r^f$ nor $x^e$ need move.

So the issue comes down to one of *substitutability* in the portfolios of private asset holders.[41] If, say, U.S. and Japanese government debt instruments are perfect substitutes, then sterilized intervention cannot move the dollar/yen exchange rate at all. If they are very strong but not quite perfect substitutes, it cannot move the exchange rate much. But if the two types of bonds are rather imperfect substitutes, there is real scope for exchange rate intervention to work.

Which theoretical case is most relevant to the real world? In truth, most economists are skeptical that sterilized interventions either *should* work in principle or *do* work in practice. Some (not including me) elevate this belief to a quasi-religious status. Substitutability is almost perfect, they insist. And a central bank's foreign exchange portfolio is so small relative to even the *daily* volume of foreign exchange transactions that it can do little more than spit in the ocean.

Take these two arguments in turn, starting with perfect substitutability. I do not believe that, say, Bill Gates is indifferent to whether his portfolio includes $10 billion of U.S. Treasury bills or $10 billion worth of Japanese government bills. Even if the *expected* returns are identical (as uncovered interest parity suggests), the risk characteristics are quite different.

But the point about magnitudes is even more apposite, I think, and it may go a long way toward explaining why official interventions seem to have such small effects. Rarely do central banks intervene on the scale that would be necessary to move what have become truly enormous markets in the major currencies: the dollar, the yen, and the euro. With typical interventions of $1 or $2 billion in a foreign exchange market that routinely handles over a *trillion* dollars each day, it is hardly surprising that central bank operations do not move markets very much. In what market does a 0.1 percent change in supply move the price notably?

In fact, the amazing thing may be that such small interventions move markets at all. A decade or so ago, the weight of the academic evidence clearly held that they did not—that sterilized intervention was ineffective.[42] But studies of the 1970s and 1980s may have been hampered by the lack of detailed data on the exact timing and magnitude of interventions. More recent studies, published in the 1990s, find more evidence that intervention works, at least somewhat.[43]

To be sure, it would be foolish for any modern central bank in a country with a floating exchange rate to believe that it has tight control over its currency value—whether via sterilized intervention or otherwise. Market folk wisdom holds, variously, that you shouldn't stand in front of a speeding freight train or try to catch a falling knife. (But it also holds, Don't fight the Fed. Oh, well. Who ever said that markets were consistent?) No sensible person believes that small-scale foreign exchange interventions can reverse the direction of a big market that is hell-bent on moving in a particular direction. That *is*, indeed, tantamount to standing in front of a speeding freight train.

But market participants do not always hold strong convictions about which way the exchange rate should go. After a big run-up, for example, traders may become nervous that the dollar (or the yen or the euro) is overbought and is therefore due for a "correction." Under such circumstances, a loud, clear intervention by the authorities, especially if concerted and sprung as a surprise, may succeed in pushing the market around without committing terribly much money. On those rare occasions when markets are not united in their view of the direction in which the exchange rate should be going, but governments are (and they show it), official intervention may be able to influence exchange rates substantially.[44] The Plaza Accord in 1985 may have been one such example. Robert Rubin's successful turnaround of the dollar in 1995 may have been another.

My second obvious point is that not all markets are very deep. A $1-billion intervention in dollar/yen may, under most circumstances, be a futile gesture. But if $1 billion is applied to the cross-rate between, say, the British pound and the Czech crown, it may look like the Czech authorities have brought out the heavy artillery. I am concerned that too many governments of (economically) small countries may be afraid of adopting a floating exchange rate in part because they think that any subsequent intervention efforts are doomed to failure. That may not be so. No one will expect them to be able to move the dollar/yen exchange rate.

To return to our main theme, a modern central bank might well question how much wisdom is embodied in foreign exchange markets that can't even get uncovered interest parity right as an *ex ante* relationship—that is, as a way to forecast exchange rate movements. Nor need the central banks of the world feel tightly constrained by uncovered interest parity in an *ex post* sense. Puzzling as it may be, exchange rates and interest rates seem to lead separate lives.

## Summing Up

I can review, encapsulate, and perhaps integrate the main messages of this chapter by pointing out the shortcomings of a straw man. Imagine a central bank so enraptured by modern thinking that it dutifully follows the signals emitted by the financial markets. This hypothetical (and, you might say, wimpy!) central bank would read what the markets expect it to do from the term structure of interest rates, from prices observed in the federal funds futures market and, perhaps, from the foreign exchange markets. Then it would deliver precisely that policy. Monetary policy decisions would effectively be privatized.

What's wrong with such a system? Many things. To start in a strictly rational expectations framework, following the markets in this way can lead to a kind of "dog chasing its tail" phenomenon that may not have a well-defined equilibrium. At the very least, it is likely to produce excessively volatile monetary policy and therefore excessively volatile markets. This is perhaps the most fundamental criticism of the strategy of following the markets.

Now allow a few not-so-rational, but probably quite realistic, elements to creep into the story. A central bank that tries too hard to please currency and bond traders may wind up adopting the market's ludicrously short effective time horizons as its own—thereby succumbing to the very danger that central bank independence was supposed to guard against.

And then there are those allegedly invaluable signals from the all-knowing financial markets. According to the predominant economic theory, the term structure embodies the best possible forecasts of future short rates and thus the best possible forecasts of what the market thinks the central bank will (or is it should?) do. In practice, however, forecasts of future short rates derived from the term structure prove to be wide of the mark—perhaps because of myopia, or perhaps for other reasons. At the very least, the collective wisdom that is supposedly embodied in the term structure appears to be greatly overrated.

A market-friendly central bank is also informed, and supposedly constrained, by uncovered interest parity, which links short-term interest rates tightly to near-term exchange rate expectations. Look up the expected dollar/euro exchange rate and the European interest rate, and the market will tell you what the corresponding U.S. interest rate should be. But once again, this source of market wisdom fails the empirical test. Its implied exchange rate forecasts err badly. Odd as it may seem, interest rate differentials and exchange rates frequently go their own ways.

The upshot of all this is that it may not be wise for a central bank to take its marching orders from the markets. But that does not mean that modern central bankers should emulate King Canute and pretend they can command the markets. Plainly, they cannot. Rather, an astute central banker nowadays should view the markets as a powerful herd that is sometimes right, sometimes wrong, always a force to be reckoned with, but sometimes manipulable. Most fundamentally, the markets need to be led, not followed.

For a central bank to be the leader, it must set out on a sensible and comprehensible course—or else the putative followers may refuse to fall in line. Furthermore, being transparent about its goals and its methods should help the central bank assume this leadership role by teaching the markets where and how it wants to lead them.

We have thus come full circle. The greater transparency explained and extolled in chapter 1 should, it appears, help put the monetary authorities in the position of leader, rather than follower. It's a nice symbiosis—or, as Shakespeare once put it, "a consummation devoutly to be wished."

# Appendix to Chapter 3:
# The Expectations Theory of
# the Term Structure

Start with the two-period example mentioned in the text. Arbitrage implies that, ignoring possible risk or liquidity premiums, the two-period interest factor must be the *product* of today's one-period interest factor and the one-period interest factor *expected* to prevail one period from now:

$$(3.6) \qquad (1 + r_{2,t})^2 = (1 + r_{1,t})(1 + r^e_{1,t+1}).$$

Here $r_i$ is the i-period interest rate (expressed at an annual rate), t measures time, and the superscript e indicates an expectation.

Proceeding similarly, the three-period interest factor should be the product of today's one-period interest factor and the next *two* expected one-period factors:

$$(1 + r_{3,t})^3 = (1 + r_{1,t})(1 + r^e_{1,t+1})(1 + r^e_{1,t+2}),$$

and so on—except for possible term premiums—for longer maturities. By (3.6), this last expression can be written more compactly as

$$(3.7) \qquad (1 + r_{3,t})^3 = (1 + r_{2,t})^2 (1 + r^e_{1,t+2}),$$

which relates the current two-period and three-period interest rates.

Because both $r_{2,t}$ and $r_{3,t}$ are observable, equations like (3.7) can be used to deduce the implied forward rates mentioned in the text, although the actual calculations are bedeviled by the question of how to handle term premiums. For example, ignoring any term premiums:

$$(1 + r^e_{1,t+2}) = (1 + r_{3,t})^3 / (1 + r_{2,t})^2$$

In words, the one-period interest factor expected to prevail two periods from now is the ratio of the three-period interest factor divided by the two-period factor.

The corresponding equation for nine- and ten-year bonds is

(3.8) $$(1 + r^e_{1,t+9}) = (1 + r_{10,,t})^{10} / (1 + r_{9,,t})^9 .$$

If we take logs of (3.8) and use the standard approximation $\log(1+r) \approx r$, we get equation (3.3) in the text. The corresponding linear regression alluded to in the text is

$$r_{1,t+9} = a + b(r^e_{1,t+9}) + e_t = a + b(10r_{10,t} - 9r_{9,t}) + e_t,$$

and, as reported, estimating this equation leads to a resounding rejection of the null hypothesis $b = 1$.

# Conclusion:
# Thoroughly Modern Central Banking

Inertia has always been a powerful force in the staid world of central banking, and it still is. So rapid change in the ways in which monetary policy is conducted and in which central banks are managed should be neither expected nor desired. There are good reasons, some of which I have mentioned in this book, for central banks to resist the latest fads and fancies. Yet motion in several more modern directions has been palpable in recent years—even if it proceeds at a glacial pace. Hence the phrase "quiet revolution."

The three aspects of change in modern central banking that strike me as most noteworthy have been featured in this book. Loosely speaking, in the older tradition, monetary policy was made by a single, secretive central banker who harbored a rather imperious attitude toward the markets. In stark contrast, in the newer tradition, monetary policy is made by a transparent monetary policy committee that pays rapt attention to market signals. Those of you who have come this far will know that I view each of these three transformations of central banking as steps up the evolutionary chain—but with certain exceptions.

Greater transparency, the subject of chapter 1, is the area in which the quiet revolution has progressed the fastest—and with the most obviously salutary results for the practice of monetary policy. Change over the past decade or so has been at a breathtaking pace, by the normal glacial standards of central banks. And I venture to guess that it will be just as fast over the next decade. Societies everywhere are becoming more open, and central bankers will be unable to resist the historical tide—if indeed they try. The public should be applauding and encouraging the current trend toward greater central bank transparency, for central bankers, being shy folks by nature, often need to be prodded to move into the sunlight.

The second trend—away from individual decision makers and toward committees—is also quite notable, although the Federal Reserve and the Bundesbank (the predecessor of the ECB) arrived there decades ago. It has been a stealth revolution, rarely commented upon by academic observers. And, ironically, it is almost complete. In this sphere, the reasons for change are far less obvious and are hardly ever discussed by either theorists or practitioners; so I have tried to elucidate them in chapter 2. Briefly, they come down to risk aversion—that is, "Don't put all society's eggs into one central banker's basket"—and the belief that collective wisdom may be superior to individual wisdom. Since relatively few central banks still leave monetary policy decisions in the hands of a lone-wolf governor, this trend cannot have much further to go. One interesting question, however, is whether the Federal Open Market Committee will become more democratic once Alan Greenspan retires. I suspect it will.

Finally, I have noted in chapter 3 that thoroughly modern central banks increasingly take not only information, but sometimes also advice, from the financial markets. Taking information is all to the good, in my view; indeed, it is essential to proper central banking practice in a market-dominated world. But taking advice holds some dangers against which astute central bankers must be ever on guard. While a committee may be expected to outperform an individual, there is no reason to think that a *herd* will do even better—even if members of the herd wear Hermes ties and take home seven-figure salaries. A truly modern, but still wise, central banker must learn to harvest the wheat from the markets and discard the chaff. Going modern need not and should not mean relinquishing the role of leader to the financial markets. Monetary policy decisions are, in the end, *public policy* decisions and, as such, are not suitable candidates for privatization.

# Notes

Introduction

1. See Shiller (2000).

2. Brunner (1981), 5. I first encountered this quotation in a notable paper by Goodfriend (1986), which was way ahead of its time.

3. The Okun Lectures were delivered in April 2002.

4. Blinder et al. (2001), 1.

Chapter 1. Through the Looking Glass

1. Alan Greenspan, "The Economy," Remarks at the Bay Area Council Conference, San Francisco, January 11, 2002.

2. Quoted in Fischer (1990), 1181.

3. The case for central bank independence is explored at length in Blinder (1998, chapter 3) and in many other places. I will not dwell on this subject here.

4. The presidents of the twelve reserve banks are not political appointees, however. They are appointed by their respective boards of directors, with the approval of the Board of Governors in Washington.

5. In Blinder (1998), 64.

6. I am talking, of course, about *nominal* interest rates. In the long run, monetary policy may not be able to influence *real* interest rates much, if at all. But in the short run, observed changes in nominal rates—especially those at the short end of the yield curve—are probably mostly changes in real rates.

7. This point is rarely noticed. Any long-term interest rate can be decomposed into a sequence of expected future one-day rates, plus a term premium. Those expected one-day rates should, in principle, be fully determined by future monetary policy. Any other influence on long-term rates, such as expected

inflation or expected future budget deficits, presumably works its will through future monetary policy.

8. In many theoretical models, the expected rate of inflation will "jump" in response to credible central bank pronouncements. But I remain dubious about this as a characterization of reality.

9. See Blinder (2000), 1422.

10. The ones ranked higher were having a history of living up to its words, central bank independence, and having a history of fighting inflation. The ones ranked lower were fiscal discipline by the government, imposing constraints by a rule, and offering personal incentives for the central banker to keep inflation low.

11. Most economists would say that the mandate embodies two goals, not three, because price stability more or less guarantees "moderate long-term [nominal] interest rates."

12. A lengthy discussion of the Fed's long-term inflation goal at the July 1996 FOMC meeting showed considerable sentiment for a target around 2 percent. However, no explicit goal was adopted. See the transcript of the July 2–3, 1996, FOMC meeting, 41ff.

13. One reason: The unemployment rate is not the only factor relevant to whether inflation goes up or down.

14. See, for example, Svensson (1997).

15. See, for example, Ferguson (2002), 6.

16. In long-run forecasting, the assumption that nominal interest rates are constant while inflation is drifting up or down can also lead to dynamic instability as the real rate moves away from equilibrium. So a constant *real* rate assumption may be better.

17. It is noteworthy that the RBNZ is one of the few central banks in which decision making still rests in the hands of an individual rather than a committee.

18. See Blinder (1998), 13–18.

19. Greenspan (1989), 49 and 50.

20. Greenspan (1989), 70.

21. The Bank of Japan's new policy is to do so with a ten-year delay, but that has not started yet.

22. The rest of this section is adapted from Blinder et al., (2001),37–38.

23. The following distinction and the nomenclature come from Blinder et al. (2001), especially chapter 4.

24. The Bank of Canada has a small committee, but it consists of the governor and his two top deputies, and it has no statutory authority.

25. *De jure,* the FOMC makes decisions by majority vote. De facto, however, one can argue that the dominance of Alan Greenspan is so great that monetary policy is, in effect, made by a single person.

26. As mentioned, the ECB denies that it even takes votes. It can be argued

that moving beyond a statement of the numerical vote to identifying the votes of each member might subject committee members to political pressure.

27. They have been particularly rare on the Greenspan Fed. Over the two full years 2000–01, for example, covering nineteen FOMC meetings (including three teleconferences), there were only three recorded dissents.

28. See Clare and Courtenay (2001). It should be noted that the MPC's votes are reported in the minutes. It could be that the market reaction is just to the numerical vote, not to the words.

29. See Eijffinger and Geraats (2002), 20.

30. The other central banks studied were the Fed, the ECB, the Bank of Japan, and the Swiss National Bank.

31. In principle, the Fed could make the switch with no change in its legal mandate. But I believe that the Fed would seek legislative authority for such a major change.

32. For more on this issue, see Blinder and Yellen (2001).

33. See, for example, Svensson (1997). In truth, however, the concerns about employment are typically unstated and often hidden—a clear violation of transparency.

34. See Orphanides (2000).

35. In this context, price-level targeting may have an advantage over inflation targeting. See, for example, Wolman (1998) or Svensson (1999).

36. The inflation targeter's reply is that deflation will never occur with proper application of inflation targeting and a target safely above zero.

37. Eijffinger and Geraats (2002) rank the Fed (tied for) fifth out of nine major central banks.

38. For a comprehensive list of changes at the Fed in the direction of greater transparency, see Blinder et al. (2001), section 5.1, or Poole et al. (2001).

Chapter 2. *Ex Uno Plures*

1. As I suggested in chapter 1, many observers would put Canada, rather than Norway, in this category. That would still leave the count at two.

2. See Blinder (1995), lecture II, 28–31. These lectures were subsequently expanded into the Robbins Lectures at the London School of Economics in 1996 and published as Blinder (1998).

3. There is one exception: Standard economics allows for different preferences across committee members. More on this below.

4. However, Morris and Shin (2002) argue that the existence of private information may influence the way public information (such as central bank announcements) affects markets.

5. Economic theory does include a budding literature on "bounded rationality" that recognizes such limits. But there have been few applications of

bounded rationality to monetary policy making. See, for example, Sargent (1999) and some of his subsequent work.

6. The operational verb here is "should." Press reports regularly suggest systematic hawk–dove differences.

7. There is some evidence that the district bank presidents are, on average, more hawkish than the Washington-based governors, who are political appointees. See, for example, Meade and Sheets (2002) and a number of the references therein.

8. Pooling can mean either averaging or deciding by majority vote. Gerlach-Kristen (2001) shows that averaging is better when members are of equal ability, but voting is better when abilities on the committee are unequal.

9. Some readers may be thinking about the Fed's conversion to monetarism in 1979–82. Wasn't that an idiosyncratic theory? My answer is that neither Paul Volcker nor the FOMC as a whole ever truly embraced monetarism. Volcker found it a convenient "cover story" for the excruciatingly tight monetary policy that he knew he would have to pursue.

10. Alan Greenspan has chaired the FOMC for about sixteen years and has never been on the losing side of a vote. Nor has he ever eked out a close victory.

11. See Chappell, McGregor, and Vermilyea (2001), especially table 4. Their regressions attribute roughly 50 percent of the decision-making weight to Burns, leaving the other 50 percent for the other eleven FOMC voters.

12. See, for example, Davis (1992) or Sorkin et al. (2001).

13. For more details, see Blinder and Morgan (2004). That paper reports on two very different experiments that yielded almost identical results. I describe only the monetary policy experiment here, but there was also a purely statistical experiment (an urn problem) devoid of economic content.

14. A notable exception is Fehr and Tyran (2001).

15. Unlike real-world MPCs, these committees had no designated leaders.

16. For example, Ball (1999) and Rudebusch and Svensson (1999).

17. The charge was assessed *only* in the quarter of the interest rate change.

18. I mean "excessive" in the sense that no central bank constantly pushes rates up and down to see what happens.

19. It was clear from observing the experiments, however, that the groups took more clock time.

20. As mentioned in note 13, we also conducted a purely statistical experiment devoid of economic content. In that experiment, too, groups did better and were not slower in reaching decisions.

21. The apparently sexist pronoun reflects an underlying empirical regularity: Nearly all heads of central banks to date have been men.

22. Yet the theoretical gains from pooling knowledge (e.g., Gerlach-Kristen (2001)) or from using diverse decision heuristics (e.g., Hong and Page [1998]) are presumably available to either individualistic or collegial committees.

23. In the case of voting on the short-term interest rate, it seems reasonable

to expect single-peaked preferences to be the norm—and they probably are. But I can remember cases on the FOMC in which, say, a member preferred either 0 or 50 basis points to a 25-basis-point move that would look like a weak compromise.

24. The MPC does, however, make its reasoning clear in the minutes, which follow less than two weeks after each meeting.

25. The neutral real interest rate is defined as the real rate at which inflation is neither rising nor falling. See Blinder (1998, 31–33).

26. The quadratic loss functions that are ubiquitous in economic theory make computations too hard. We used absolute values with equal weights to make it easy for subjects to compute losses in their heads.


Chapter 3. Following the Leader

1. See, among others, Cukierman (1992), Debelle and Fischer (1995), and McCallum (1997).

2. See, for example, Fischer (1994) or Eijffinger and De Haan (1996).

3. See Posen (1993) or Campillo and Miron (1997).

4. I first raised this danger in Blinder (1995).

5. For example, a few observers have gone so far as to claim that central banks should simply let markets determine interest rates. See, for example, Ely (1998). Fortunately, this is not the dominant view.

6. On herding, see, for example, Banerjee (1992) and Scharfstein and Stein (1990). On overreaction, see Shiller (1979, 1981) and Gilles and LeRoy (1991).

7. I have tried several times to track this quotation down. Several of Black's friends remember hearing him say it, but none have been able to point me to a published source.

8. Bikhchandani and Sharma (2000) is a useful survey which helped inform the next few paragraphs.

9. Bikhchandani and Sharma (2000) cite five scholarly papers dated between 1995 and 1999.

10. Most empirical studies seem to use the measure devised by Lakonishok, Shleifer, and Vishny (1992).

11. Regarding fads, see Shiller (1984, 2000). Regarding bubbles, see Flood and Garber (1980) and West (1987). Garber (2000) reminds us that we should not be too quick to declare a bubble.

12. For example, in Blinder (1998), 61.

13. This statement assumes risk neutrality.

14. One possibility (which I owe to Christopher Sims): If the short-term interest rate literally follows a first-order autoregressive process (so that only its own lagged value matters), an interest-rate shock today will move the *expectations* of *all* future short rates, making the short rate and the implied forward rates perfectly correlated. But the correlation drops away from 1.0 as more lags and/or more variables are added.

15. The thorough Fed staff calculated this correlation for several earlier years as well. Sometimes it was higher than 0.54, sometimes lower.

16. The word "roughly" refers to the fact that the approximation log(1+x) ≈ x is used. See the appendix to this chapter.

17. This equality ignores any possible risk or liquidity premiums, which are mentioned below.

18. The yield curve is a graph relating the rate of interest to the maturity of the instrument.

19. This account leaves out the aforementioned term premium, which is what makes such exercises complicated.

20. Two useful references are Shiller (1990) and Campbell (1995).

21. The data come from McCulloch and Kwon (1993).

22. The line is not forced to go through the origin to allow for different term premiums on nine-year and ten-year bonds.

23. The estimate of the standard error uses the Newey-West correction.

24. If that sounds complicated, see Campbell (1995) for an explanation.

25. A plot similar to figure 3.1 for three-month and six-month Treasury bill rates using daily data from January 1982 through November 2001 (not shown here) looks much better. It appears that the expectations theory works better at the very short end of the yield curve.

26. Chow's (1989) long rate was twenty years; his short rate was one month; and his sample was monthly U.S. data from 1959 to 1983.

27. The long-run asymptotic effect is 97 basis points, insignificantly different from 100.

28. In this case, the long-run asymptotic effect is 106 basis points.

29. There is a bright side, however. If myopia leads the markets to overreact to the central bank's decisions, the power and speed of monetary policy will thereby be enhanced.

30. Purists will note that $E(1/X)$ is not equal to $1/E(X)$, which is one reason for the word "approximately." But it has never been clear—at least to me—what to make of this Jensen's inequality problem, for while the American investor presumably cares about $E(1/X)$, the German investor presumably cares about $E(X)$.

31. Once again, there are potential complications owing to such things as liquidity premia. These are relevant to *levels* but should mostly wash out when we deal with *changes*.

32. Over durations and currencies for which forward markets exist, there is a version of (3.4) called *covered interest rate parity*. Unlike its uncovered brother, covered interest rate parity *must* hold because people can actually carry out all the necessary transactions to ensure that the arbitrage relation holds.

33. His regressions pertain to the following exchange rates: pound/DM, dollar/pound, pound/French franc, pound/yen, dollar/DM, $/yen, and DM/yen. They all end in December 1998, and they begin at various dates from January 1976 to October 1978.

34. See Goodman (1979). See also Taylor (1997), which is a summary of a special issue of the *International Journal of Finance and Economics* devoted to technical analysis.

35. See, for example, Meredith and Chinn (1998).

36. Meredith (2001) and Alquist and Chinn (2002) both emphasize the roles of productivity and profitability in attracting foreign capital. But there is still a leap to connect capital *inflows* to *expansionary* monetary policy.

37. See Kenen (2001), 55–56.

38. Interest rate parity, whether covered or uncovered, reminds us that such an operation may have implications for foreign interest rates.

39. By contrast, an *unsterilized* intervention (e.g., buying a foreign bond and paying for it with newly created high-powered money) should move both the exchange rate and the domestic interest rate.

40. This leaves out the logical possibility that today's exchange rate and tomorrow's *expected* exchange move up or down in proportion, leaving $x^e$ unchanged. But in that case, one wonders what will ultimately happen to the country's current account balance.

41. There are other mechanisms via which economists have sometimes argued that sterilized interventions might work—for example, if forex operations *signal* future changes in (domestic) monetary policy. This mechanism muddies the waters, in my view, because it argues that *sterilized* interventions create expectations of future *unsterilized* interventions.

42. See, for example, Edison (1993).

43. See Dominguez and Frankel (1993) and, especially, the recent survey by Sarno and Taylor (2001).

44. In support of this view, Peter Kenen (1988) found that interventions in the European Monetary System tended to be most effective when market expectations (measured by survey data) were most disperse.

# Bibliography

Alquist, Ron, and Menxie Chinn. 2002. Productivity and the euro–dollar exchange rate puzzle. NBER Working Paper no. 8824. Cambridge, Mass.: National Bureau of Economic Research.

Armstrong, J. Scott. 2001. Combining forecasts. In *Principles of Forecasting: A Handbook for Researchers and Practitioners*, ed. J. Scott Armstrong, 375–94. Boston: Kluwer Academic Publishers.

Ball, Laurence. 1999. Efficient rules for monetary policy. *International Finance* 2(1): 63–83.

Banerjee, Abhijit V. 1992. A simple model of herd behavior. *Quarterly Journal of Economics* 107(3): 797–817.

Bernanke, Ben S., Thomas Laubach, Frederic S. Mishkin, and Adam S. Posen. 1999. *Inflation Targeting: Lessons from the International Experience*. Princeton: Princeton University Press.

Bernanke, Ben S., and Michael Woodford. 1997. Inflation targets and monetary policy. *Journal of Money, Credit, and Banking* 29: 653–84.

Bikhchandani, Sushil, and Sunil Sharma. 2000. Herd behavior in financial markets: A review. *IMF Staff Papers* 47(3): 279–310. Washington, D.C.: International Monetary Fund.

Blinder, Alan S. 1995. "Central Banking in Theory and Practice." The Marshall Lectures, processed, Board of Governors of the Federal Reserve System, May 1995.

Blinder, Alan S. 1998. *Central Banking in Theory and Practice*. Cambridge, Mass: MIT Press.

———. 2000. Central bank credibility: Why do we care? How do we build it? *American Economic Review* 90(5): 1421–31.

Blinder, Alan, Charles Goodhart, Philipp Hildenbrand, David Lipton, and Charles Wyplosz. 2001. *How Do Central Banks Talk?* Geneva: International Center for Monetary and Banking Studies; London: Centre for Economic Policy Research.

Blinder, Alan S., and John Morgan. 2004. Are two heads better than one?: Monetary policy by committee. *Journal of Money, Credit, and Banking,* forthcoming.

Blinder, Alan S., and Janet L. Yellen. 2001. *The Fabulous Decade: Macroeconomic Lessons from the 1990s.* New York: Century Foundation Press.

Campbell, John Y. 1995. Some lessons from the yield curve. *Journal of Economic Perspectives* 9(3): 129–52.

Campillo, Marto, and Jeffrey A. Miron. 1997. Why does inflation differ across countries? In *Reducing Inflation: Motivation and Strategy,* ed. Christina D. Romer and David H. Romer, 335–57. Chicago: University of Chicago Press.

Chappell, Henry W., Rob Roy McGregor, and Todd Vermilyea. 2001. Models of monetary policy decision-making: Arthur Burns and the Federal Open Market Committee. Columbia: University of South Carolina. Working Paper.

Chow, Gregory C. 1989. Rational versus adaptive expectations in present value models. *Review of Economics and Statistics* 71(3): 376–84.

Clare, Andrew, and Roger Courtenay. 2001. Assessing the impact of macroeconomic news announcements on securities prices over different monetary policy regimes. Working Paper no. 125. London: Bank of England.

Cukierman, Alex. 1992. *Central Bank Strategy, Credibility and Independence: Theory and Evidence.* Cambridge, Mass.: MIT Press.

———. 1998. The economics of central banking. In *Contemporary Economic Issues, Proceedings of the Eleventh World Congress of the International Economic Association, Tunis,* ed. Holger C. Wolf, 5(125): 37–82. New York: St. Martin's Press; London: Macmillan Press.

Debelle, Guy, and Stanley Fischer. 1995. How independent should a central bank be? In *Goals, Guidelines and Constraints Facing Monetary Policy Makers,* ed. Jeffrey C. Fuhrer, 38: 195–221. Boston: Federal Reserve Bank of Boston.

Dominguez, Kathryn M., and Jeffrey A. Frankel. 1993. *Does Foreign Exchange Intervention Work?* Washington: Institute for International Economics.

Edison Hali J. 1993. The effectiveness of central-bank intervention: A survey of the literature after 1982. Special Papers in International Economics no. 18. Princeton: International Finance Section, Princeton University.

Eijffinger, Sylvester, and Jakob De Haan. 1996. The political economy of central-bank independence. Special Papers in International Economics no. 19. Princeton: International Finance Section, Princeton University.

Eijffinger, Sylvester, and Petra Geraats. 2002. How transparent are central banks? Working Paper no. 3188. London: Centre for Economic Policy Research.

Ely, Bert. 1998. Leave interest rates to the market place. *Financial Times,* September 12, 1998. Available at *www.ely–co.com.*

Faust, Jon. 1996. Whom can we trust to run the Fed? Theoretical support for the founders' views. *Journal of Monetary Economics* 37(2): 267–83.

Fehr, Ernst, and Jean Robert Tyran. 2001. Does money illusion matter? *American Economic Review* 91(5): 1239–62.

Ferguson Roger W. 2002. Why central banks should talk. Speech delivered to the Graduate Institute of International Studies, Switzerland on January 8, 2002.

Fischer, Stanley. 1990. Rules versus discretion in monetary policy. In *Handbook of Monetary Economics*, ed. Benjamin M. Friedman and Frank H. Hahn, 2(8): 1155–84. Amsterdam: North Holland.

———. 1994. Modern central banking. In *The Future of Central Banking: The tercentenary symposium of the Bank of England*, ed. Forrest Capie et al., 262–308. Cambridge: Cambridge University Press.

Flood, Robert P., and Peter M. Garber. 1980. Market fundamentals versus price-level bubbles: The first tests. *Journal of Political Economy* 88(4): 745–70.

Garber, Peter M. 2000. *Famous First Bubbles: The Fundamentals of Early Manias.* Cambridge, Mass.: MIT Press.

Gerlach–Kristen, Petra. 2001. Monetary policy committees and interest-rate setting. Basel: University of Basel. Working Paper.

Gilles, Christian, and Stephen F. LeRoy. 1991. Econometric aspects of the variance-bounds tests: A survey. *Review of Financial Studies* 4(4): 753–91.

Goodfriend, Marvin. 1986. Monetary mystique: Secrecy and central banking. *Journal of Monetary Economics* 17(1): 63–92.

Goodman Stephen H. 1979. Foreign exchange rate forecasting techniques: Implications for business and policy. *Journal of Finance* 34(2): 415–27.

Greenspan, Alan. 1989. Statement and additional material in hearing before the Subcommittee on Domestic Monetary Policy of the Committee on Banking, Finance and Urban Affairs, House of Representatives, One Hundred First Congress on October 25, 1989.

———. 2002. The Economy. Speech delivered to the Bay Area Council conference, San Francisco, on January 11, 2002.

Hong, Lu, and Scott E. Page. 1998. Diversity and optimality, processed, Syracuse University.

J. P. Morgan. 2000. *Guide to Central Bank Watching*. New York.

Kenen, Peter B. 1988. *Managing Exchange Rates*. London: Routledge.

———. 2001. *The International Architecture: What's New? What's Missing?* Washington, D.C.: Institute for International Economics.

Lakonishok, Josef, Andrei Shleifer, and Robert W. Vishny. 1992. The impact of institutional trading on stock prices. *Journal of Financial Economics* 32(1): 23–43.

McCallum, Bennett T. 1997. Crucial issues concerning central bank independence. *Journal of Monetary Economics* 39(1): 99–112.

Meade, Ellen E., and D. Nathan Sheets. 2002. Regional influences on U.S. monetary policy: Some implications for Europe. Center for Economic Performance Working Paper. London: London School of Economics and Political Science.

Meredith, Guy. 2001. Why has the euro been so weak? IMF Working Paper no. 155. Washington, D.C.: International Monetary Fund.

Meredith, Guy, and Menzie D. Chinn. 1998. Long-horizon uncovered interest rate parity. NBER Working Paper no. 6797. Cambridge, Mass.: National Bureau of Economic Research.

Meese, Richard A., and Kenneth Rogoff. 1983. Empirical exchange rate models of the seventies: Do they fit out of sample? *Journal of International Economics* 14(1–2): 3–24.

Meyer, Laurence H. 2001. Inflation targets and inflation targeting. Speech delivered to the University of California at San Diego on July 17, 2001.

McCulloch, J. Huston, and Heon-Chul Kwon. 1993. U.S. term structure data 1947–1991. Working Paper no. 93–6. Columbus: Ohio State University.

Morris, Stephen, and Hyun Song Shin. 2002. "Social Value of Public Information." *American Economic Review* 92(5): 1521–34.

Orphanides, Athanasios. 2000. The quest for prosperity without inflation. European Central Bank Working Paper no. 15. Frankfurt: European Central Bank.

Poole, William, Robert H. Rasche, and Daniel L. Thornton. 2001. Market anticipations of monetary policy actions. St. Louis: Federal Reserve Bank of St. Louis. Mimeograph.

Posen, Adam S. 1993. Why central bank independence does not cause low inflation: There is no institutional fix for politics. In *Finance and the International Economy*, ed. Richard O'Brien, 7: 41–54. Oxford: Oxford University Press.

Rogoff, Kenneth S. 1985. The optimal degree of commitment to an intermediate monetary target. *Quarterly Journal of Economics* 100(4): 1169–89.

Romer, Christina D., and David H. Romer. 2000. Federal Reserve information and the behavior of interest rates. *American Economic Review* 90(3): 429–57.

Rudebusch, Glenn D., and Lars E. O. Svensson. 1999. Policy rules for inflation targeting. In *Monetary Policy Rules*, ed. John B. Taylor, 203–46. NBER Conference Report series. Chicago: University of Chicago Press.

Sargent, Thomas J. 1999. *The Conquest of American Inflation*. Princeton: Princeton University Press.

Sarno, Lucio, and Mark P. Taylor. 2001. Official intervention in the foreign exchange market: Is it effective and, if so, how does it work? *Journal of Economic Literature* 39(3): 839–68.

Scharfstein, David S., and Jeremy C. Stein. 1990. Herd behavior and investment. *American Economic Review* 80(3): 465–79.

Shiller, Robert J. 1979. The volatility of long-term interest rates and expectations models of the term structure. *Journal of Political Economy* 87(6): 1190–1219.

———. 1981. Do stock prices move too much to be justified by subsequent changes in dividends? *American Economic Review* 71(3): 421–36.

———. 1984. Stock prices and social dynamics. *Brookings Papers on Economic Activity* (2): 457–98. Washington, D.C.: Brookings Institution.

———. 1990. The term structure of interest rates. In *Handbook of Monetary Economics*, ed. Benjamin M. Friedman and Frank H. Hahn, 1(8): 627–72. Amsterdam: North-Holland.

——. 2000. *Irrational Exuberance*. Princeton: Princeton University Press.

Sibert, Anne C. 2001. Monetary policy committees: Individual and collective reputations. London: Birkbeck College, University of London. Working Paper.

Sorkin, Robert D., Christopher J. Hays, and Ryan West. 2001. Signal-detection analysis of group decision-making. *Psychological Review* 108(1): 183–203.

Svensson, Lars E. O. 1997. Optimal inflation targets, "conservative" central banks, and linear inflation contracts. *American Economic Review* 87(1): 98–114.

——. 1999. Price-level targeting versus inflation targeting: A free lunch? *Journal of Money, Credit and Banking* 31(3): 277–95.

Taylor, Mark P. 1997. Editor's introduction. *International Journal of Finance and Economics* 2(1): 263–66.

Wadhwani, Sushil B. 1999. Currency puzzles. Speech delivered to the London School of Economics on September 16, 1999. London: Bank of England.

Waller, Christopher J. 1992. A bargaining model of partisan appointments to the central bank. *Journal of Monetary Economics* 29(3): 411–28.

West, Kenneth D. 1987. A specification test for speculative bubbles. *Quarterly Journal of Economics* 410(3): 553–80.

Wolman, Alexander L. 1998. Real implications of the zero bound on nominal interest rates. Computing in Economics and Finance Working Paper no. 1152. Chestnut Hill, Mass.: Society for Computational Economics, Boston College.

# Index